Psychological Counseling in a Small College

by

EUGENIA HANFMANN
RICHARD M. JONES
ELLIOT BAKER

Brandeis Psychological Counseling Center

and

LEO KOVAR

formerly psychiatrist at Brandeis University

With an Introduction by
LAWRENCE K. FRANK

SCHENKMAN PUBLISHING COMPANY, INC.
Cambridge, Massachusetts

Copyright © 1963

SCHENKMAN PUBLISHING COMPANY, INC.
CAMBRIDGE 38, MASSACHUSETTS

Printed in the United States of America

All rights reserved. This book, or parts thereof, may not be reproduced in any form without written permission of the publishers.

CONTENTS

INTRODUCTION *Lawrence K. Frank* v

PREFACE vii

CHAPTER I Organization of a Counseling Service in a Small College: *Eugenia Hanfmann* 1

CHAPTER II Establishing a Psychiatric Service in a College: *Leo Kovar* 27

CHAPTER III Specific Features of Therapeutic Work on a Small Campus: *Eugenia Hanfmann, Elliot Baker, Richard M. Jones* 43

CHAPTER IV The Relation of Psychology Courses to Counseling: *Richard M. Jones* 101

CONCLUDING REMARKS 117

INTRODUCTION

The present prospect of rapidly increasing numbers of college students has brought a variety of estimates as to the additional buildings and equipment and enlarged faculties needed for these students. But little account has been taken of the equally pressing requirements for counseling services for these new members of our academic communities.

Tomorrow many adolescents will be entering college with few family traditions relevant to the demands and opportunities for college living and study; they will be confronted with the many confusions and complexities which even the most normal and "well adjusted" student must face. Suddenly released from family supervision and exposed to the demands and the expectations not only of faculty but of other students, every student must find his or her own course, resolving what Erikson has called the "identity crisis" and the inevitable conflicts between impulses and aspirations. It is indeed remarkable how often wise and judicious counseling enables students to cope with these life tasks effectively, with minimal liability to academic failure and to persistent personality problems.

It will be an ironic victory if, as a nation, we provide the buildings, equipment, and faculty for this coming influx of students, but allow these students to struggle unaided with the recurrent perplexities and personality handicaps by which so many are defeated. This is liable to happen, however, unless we recognize that all students, not just a few, are involved in these adolescent problems which they must encounter and solve on the road to adult maturity.

This volume, therefore, is of large import since it tells how psychological counseling was developed in a small college, namely at Brandeis University, on a basis that has made this service available to all those who need it. In describing how the staff gradually evolved the basic principles and policies for their relations with the students, with the administrative offices, and with the students' parents, the writers have been unusually candid: they have reviewed not only the successful steps but also those that proved undesirable or ineffective and had to be altered, so that the reader can participate vicariously in the gradual and sometimes painful process of developing a counseling service.

An effective counseling service for students must be provided by all our colleges since it is essential for the achievement of the academic goals they are seeking to attain. As a guide to the establishment and operation of such a service this volume will provide the fruits of many years of exploration and testing of procedures that will satisfy high professional requirements and serve the exigent human needs of young men and women today. As the writers state in the preface, this book is directed to "all those who are actively involved either in on-going mental health work in colleges or in attempts to introduce or extend such work, including both professional workers in the field and educational administrators." It may also be warmly recommended to all the helping professions, social work, school counselors and guidance workers, college and university chaplains, and the increasing number of clergymen who are accepting the responsibilities of "pastoral psychology."

LAWRENCE K. FRANK

PREFACE[1]

The orientation of this volume is essentially pragmatic. It deals with the concrete problems involved in establishing and running a professional mental health service on a college campus. In its most general formulation the issue to which we address ourselves is that of mutual adaptation between the organizational structure of a traditional educational institution and the internal organization of the counseling process. This general issue has two aspects. As counselors or therapists we are searching for ways of making the situation of working within a school setting maximally conducive and minimally obstructive to the initiation and successful pursuit by the student of the guided process of self-discovery. This involves taking into account in the procedures of counseling the specific givens of the students' situation as distinct from the situation of clients seen in private practice or in other institutional settings. Our efforts in this respect are directed towards adapting the structure of the counseling process to the structure of student life as defined by membership in a college community. A unilateral adaptation, however, is not sufficient. An effective mental health program cannot be developed in a school setting unless the school's policies are sufficiently flexible to permit their adaptation to the basic requirements of professional counseling. All who are in-

[1] The preparation of this book was made possible by a grant made by Mr. William Heller of New York City in support of the student mental health program at Brandeis University.

volved in such enterprises learn this sooner or later, and those counseling centers and clinics that function successfully in schools are evidence of some degree of mutual adaptation. Such adaptation is usually only achieved after certain intra-institutional conflicts have been worked through and resolved. These conflicts are rarely discussed in public, particularly at the time when they are acute: the participants' personal involvement, tactical considerations and institutional loyalties impose limitations on freedom of expression. Yet a full and frank discussion of the delicate issues, both intra-institutional and inter-professional, could do much to help remove the difficulties which so often beset college counseling and which prevent many schools from starting effective mental health programs.

The content of this volume is essentially a report of the experiences of one school, Brandeis University, in working out a particular pattern of mutual adaptation between a school environment and the counseling process. Our major interest has been in working out effective counseling procedures; consequently, the major portion of the book (Chapters III and IV) is devoted to a discussion by the staff of the Counseling Center of the situational factors to which the counseling process must adapt, or which it can utilize to special advantage, and of practices which have shown promise in these respects. The problems involved in working out an organizational structure and the policies which maximally benefit a college mental health program are discussed in Chapters I and II, by the Director of the Psychological Counseling Center and by our former College Psychiatrist respectively. Although the basic issues involved in college mental health work are identical in all schools they take on different forms and offer the possibility of different solutions, depending on the characteristics of the given school setting. We consider our particular contribution to be that of exploring and formulating the possibilities for wide range mental health work which are presented by the setting of a relatively small residential

Preface

liberal arts college. We are convinced on the basis of our experience that small colleges, once they admit a mental health unit into their structure and define its function as providing direct service to the students themselves, will create rich opportunities for strategically timed psychological work which both furthers the personal development of students and enhances the achievement of general educational goals. Moreover we feel these ends to be attainable in large measure even if the school as a whole does not depart from conventional teaching methods and curricula, and even if the faculty's involvement with students is no more than average.

The audience to which the book is primarily directed consists of all those who are actively involved either in on-going mental health work in colleges or in attempts to introduce or extend such work, including both professional workers in the field and educational administrators. Insofar as we describe the modifications that are undergone by counseling work when it takes place within a specifically structured closed community our work should also be of interest to sociologists and to therapists working in other institutional settings.

We deal only tangentially with the nature of psychological problems that typically occur among college students. Furthermore, we have not aimed at an exhaustive description of the program of mental health work at Brandeis. To be complete such a report should include at the very least a description of the on-going work of Dr. Arnold Abrams, our present College Psychiatrist, and a report of the group therapy work which was started on a small scale by Dr. David Ricks two years ago; a report of the problems encountered by the current Psychiatric Consultant, Dr. Stanley Kanter, in supervising the counselors of the Center might also have thrown some light on the functioning of a therapeutic service on campus. We have also had to omit the detailed description of the ways in which the mental health services supplement on occasions other sources of student guidance, such as the faculty, the chaplains, the dormitory counselors, and the offices of the Dean of Students. The reasons for omitting from description these various aspects of our work is either that they have not been of sufficiently long duration, or else have undergone modifications through recent changes of pertinent policies or of the key personnel involved. Consequently they could not be presented in as much detail, or evaluated by us with as much confidence as can be the policies and procedures that have been developed and tested over a period of many years. One of the distinctive features of our organization is the dual administrative structure of the mental health services, with the Psychological Counseling Center attached to the Department of Psychology and the College Psychiatrist functioning as a staff member of the Health Office. This arrangement presents an opportunity for an advantageous distribution of functions and also provides a basis for a productive mode of cooperation which would be well worth describing in detail. We do not yet, however, possess sufficient data to answer the question whether the students who seek the services of the College Psychiatrist are different from those who come to the Center, in terms of the nature of initial complaints, the severity of disturbance, or other relevant features. Such data would be an essential — though not the only — factor in evaluating the merits of the "dual organization." We hope to be able to provide such data in the future.

The development of a psychological counseling program on a college campus requires the cooperation of many. We wish to express our gratitude to all those both in and out of Brandeis who have contributed to this process. Dr. Abraham Maslow has been the patron saint of the Counseling Center. He was instrumental in its establishment and has continued to act as its defender and supporter. Also the emphasis he places in his theoretical work on personal growth and on promotion of positive health as distinct from the treatment of illness has served as

Preface

a guideline for the Center's work. Of the faculty members outside our own field, Dr. Lawrence Fuchs (currently serving with the Peace Corps) has been the most active and understanding friend of the Center; he spent time and effort to acquaint the faculty with its work, and, while serving as Dean of Faculty, helped us to implement administrative arrangements that are optimal for our work. Our colleagues in the Department of Psychology, particularly the clinicians, Dr. Harry Rand and Dr. Walter Toman, could always be relied on for consultation and advice. Last but not least, we owe a debt of gratitude to President Abram Sachar whose enlightened attitude towards mental health work made our project possible, and to a succession of officers of administration who have helped us to structure our relationship to other offices in the school. Some of them were initially baffled by the policies we wished to establish, but all of them have been willing to join efforts with us in struggling to work out mutually satisfying arrangements.

The Members of the Visiting Committee to the Counseling Center which currently includes Dr. Grete Bibring, Dr. George Gardner and Dr. Stanley Kanter, have given us freely of their wide experience and have helped us to think through and to solve many of the problems that loomed large at various stages of the Center's evolution. We welcome this opportunity to express our appreciation to all of them and specifically to Dr. Bibring who has been a particularly faithful and active participant of our yearly discussion meetings.

The man whose thinking and teaching had the greatest impact on our day-to-day work with students was Dr. Andras Angyal, who for many years, until his death in 1960, served as the psychiatric consultant of the Counseling Center. Through his supervisory relationship with the counselors he has done much to shape our therapeutic work and to raise its quality. To his memory this volume is gratefully dedicated.

ORGANIZATION OF A COUNSELING SERVICE IN A SMALL COLLEGE

Eugenia Hanfmann

Although provision of modern mental health facilities to college students is a recent development, experiences in different schools justify a high positive evaluation of this adjunct to academic education. With few exceptions professional workers agree that at college age a little help goes a long way, and short therapy is the method of choice; therapists of all denominations find their most rewarding patients among college students. This is as one would expect, because the late adolescent brings to the therapeutic endeavor assets that both the younger and the older groups lack. Having passed beyond the early adolescent stage of acute conflicts and intensified defenses, he is highly motivated to come to terms with himself; he is in full possession of capacities that can be mobilized for the pursuit of self-knowledge, yet is still open and flexible enough to be able to re-organize the behavior patterns which in an older person prove very resistant to change.

The high potential for improvement is present not only in the acute disturbances of adolescence, which have a good prognosis in spite of an often turbulent picture. Neurotic personality patterns of moderate degree, the modern "character neuroses," which, because of their wide prevalence, are one of the main sources of unhappiness and inefficiency in adulthood, are also more plastic at this than at a later age, and more easily amenable to treatment. Yet exactly these people for whose future a relatively small amount of timely help would make a large difference are not likely to seek such assistance at an early stage; since their suffering is not extreme and their problems are not out of the ordinary, they will forego professional help unless it is made both easily available and socially acceptable, bearing no stigma of "abnormality." It is plausible to assume that if such conditions were created they would be taken advantage of by college students on a large scale. Such a development might become a major factor in raising the level of mental health of the adult population. Psychological counseling in colleges represents one of the most promising opportunities for doing effective preventive work.

Given this potential strategic significance of college mental health work, one wonders why it does not grow faster than it actually does, and why many schools of excellent standing still have no facilities adequate to the task. Congdon and Lothrop[1] in their survey of college counseling practices in a sample of 109 non-sectarian coeducational schools found that some psychological or psychiatric guidance was available on an organized basis (i.e. from a specially designated office) in 72% of the schools. However, such counseling was the primary task of the office in question in only 46% of the total; in the rest of the schools the emphasis was on vocational-educational advising and on testing of various kinds. If one assumes that those schools that did not return the questionnaire (20% of the selected sample) had no organized guidance facilities, it appears that only 37% of the circularized schools were sufficiently committed to meeting the emotional needs of the students to make personal counseling the primary or exclusive task of a separate office. Among the schools that did reply the percentage providing services at this level of organization varied be-

---

[1] Congdon, R. G. and Lothrop, W. W. *Survey of College Counseling Practices in the United States.* Durham, N.H.: University of New Hampshire Library (unpublished manuscript), 1961.

Organization of a Counseling Service

tween 19% for small colleges (enrollment below 2500) and 75% for large schools (enrollment above 7500).

Equally pertinent to the issue is the extent of the services provided. The data provided by the same survey on the percentage of students seen, and on the average number of interviews per student, indicate that in many schools this extent is very limited; what is probably made available is emergency help to the severely or acutely disturbed, with more intensive treatment reserved for the very few. This type of service is not likely to fulfill the significant function outlined above. While many colleges, particularly the small ones, have yet to make the first step in bringing professional mental health services to the campus, others now face the task of expanding and organizing them in a way that would make them accessible and acceptable not only to the severely disturbed minority, but also to the normal majority. The problems which this task presents in the setting of a small campus school is the topic on which the present volume is centered.

One of the major obstacles both to the introduction and to the expansion of mental health services on campus lies in the reluctance often felt by the school administration to grant the service that measure of autonomy which is a *sine qua non* of its work: the counselor must be able to withhold information from other school offices if the promise of confidentiality he gives to the student is to be valid. I shall not elaborate here on this point, which will come up repeatedly in other chapters. Rather I shall try to point out the implications which various types of administrative arrangements and various policies have for the establishment of conditions favorable for the work of a counseling center and for its acceptance by the students at large.

The school administration's wish for maintaining close contact with the counseling center, which often endangers its autonomy, is justified by the occurrence of emotional disturbances in whose handling the administration is necessarily involved; in such cases a consultation among all concerned may be clearly desirable. If one wants, however, to work largely with those students who justifiably consider themselves and their problems as normal, one must take care not to transfer to this work, inadvertently, methods adapted for dealing with the disturbed minority; manipulation of the environment has no place in the counseling of the majority of college students. Yet a tendency to such spread often makes itself felt, the more so the stronger the authoritarian or the paternalistic orientation of the school. If one grants that policies which best serve the majority (who are not likely to become a cause of serious concern to the school) are different from those needed for the disturbed minority, the problem can be formulated in this way: what kind of organizational structure and what policies can best implement principles governing therapeutic work with relatively responsible young adults without preventing a different handling of the more seriously disturbed students?

In deciding on the position of the mental health center within the administrative structure of a college one has the choice of placing it under the general jurisdiction of an administrative dean or of an academic dean. If the first alternative is chosen the service can be incorporated either with the office of student personnel or with the health service. If placed under an academic dean it will usually be associated with an academic department, that of psychology or of education; university set-ups also present the possibility of association with one of the professional schools. Another and partly related choice is whether to have the service directed and staffed by psychiatrists, or by clinical psychologists, or by members of both professions in some combination, operating either within one unit or in separate set-ups. While the decisions made on both points often depend on personal biases, availability of personnel, and other extrinsic factors, experience has shown that in different admin-

Organization of a Counseling Service

istrative structures different types of policies and practices tend to evolve. In the following, some of these trends are listed, without an attempt at completeness.

To place the student counseling center under the auspices of an administrative dean who supervises all student services seems logical from the administrative point of view; the previously quoted survey shows that *c.* two thirds of the schools still adopt this structure. Yet this arrangement may make it very difficult for the counselor to obtain and safeguard a right of privileged communication. This is particularly true if the service is closely associated with the office of student personnel or its equivalent. This office, having to deal with the students whose behavior or performance are not up to par and often cause worry, will naturally exercise a pressure for collaboration with the counseling unit. Such pressures tend to establish a mode of relationship between the two services that will keep students away from the counseling service: the fear that the fact of their attendance at a mental health center will go on their permanent record is naturally a strong deterrent for many. If the center is attached to the health office and the counselor's notes are made a part of the student's health record, the same situation holds. It is less damaging, however, because in the case of the medical service the association with the disciplinary concerns is absent. Furthermore, within this structure the administration may be more clearly aware of the professional specialized nature of the service and therefore will be less likely to attempt to shape or alter its policies.

If the counseling unit is placed within the academic structure of the school through an association with an academic department the pressures for information and for collaboration on individual cases will be less, or at least they will not come from the counselors' administrative superiors. For the rest the influence of this association on the service will depend on the orientation of the sponsoring department, usually the department of psychology. If it includes a strong clinical group many opportunities for productive cooperation will arise and its sponsorship of the service can be real and professional. By far the most important advantage of an academic connection is the possibility of attracting and keeping good clinicians by providing them with an academic position and status. In this way the core staff of the service can be made an integral part of the school; and this prevents excessive turnover which inevitably lowers the quality of counseling work.

On the other hand, if the counseling center is maintained by an academic department as a training facility for its graduate students, the consequences for its service function are not favorable. The extensive participation of beginners lowers the overall quality of the counseling work. Depending on the teachers' orientation and goals, emphasis may be placed on demonstration of dynamics at the expense of an effective exercise of therapeutic skills; selection of cases for treatment may be made in terms of training needs. Whatever the reasons, the Congdon-Lothrop survey contains indications that at those school centers functioning as training facilities for clinical psychologists or for psychiatrists, on the average a much smaller percentage of the student body is seen than at those having no such function.

Turning to the question of staffing the service, the decision to employ psychiatrists is often based on the school's concern for the proper handling of severe disturbances, and of cases with somatic involvement which require medical diagnoses. Although these cases are relatively infrequent, the risks involved in their improper handling lend great strength to this concern. On the other side of the ledger, an exclusive employment of psychiatrists precludes the extension of the mental health services to the students at large, because of the costs involved. In many schools the psychiatrically staffed units have to limit their services to consultation and referral. The psychologist, on the other hand, if he is integrated into the school's academic structure, will be paid according to the prevalent scale of academic salaries, even though he could command higher pay in other clinical installations. By a conservative estimate of the difference in the rate of pay, a psychologist in the employ of a school service will provide twice the time a psychiatrist of comparable standing would provide for the same pay; he may also prove more enduring than the psychiatrist in whose career college work is often a relatively brief episode.

In the matter of overcoming the stigma that attaches to a mental health consultation the psychologist's advantage in the school setting is probably slight; for many students it may be outweighed by the psychiatrist's greater professional prestige. One might expect those students who feel that their problems are normal to elect to see a psychologist and those who are acutely disturbed to seek out the psychiatrist; actually however, the choice will often be determined by idiosyncratic preferences and repulsions. Regardless of the initial preference, the work of any competent therapist will contribute, in time, to the diminution of the stigma, if the essential conditions of counseling are insured by the service's policies.

The obvious solution of the staffing problem is to combine the advantages presented by the employment of psychiatrists and of psychologists by employing both. The numerical ratio and the administrative framework that promotes an advantageous distribution of functions and an effective frictionless cooperation must vary depending on the size of the school and on other local conditions. In a large university it is feasible to have a mental health service staffed by both psychiatrists and psychologists and supervised by a senior psychiatrist who gives all the time that is needed for the job. In a small school this design is not practical; no school with an enrollment under 5000 is likely to adopt it, and there are at present only about forty psychiatrists in this country who work in colleges on a full time basis.[2] On the other hand, factors connected with professional prestige and with the different rate of pay militate against having psychiatrists on the staffs of services headed by psychologists. In general, in a small school it is difficult to combine members of both professions on the staff of a small counseling unit, attached either to the health office or to the department of psychology, without sacrificing the advantages presented by each type of administrative connection and without endangering the service's unified functioning. It appears wiser to maximize the different professional identities and to aim at a profitable distribution of work by having the college psychiatrist function as a staff member of the health office, cooperating closely but informally with a counseling center staffed and sponsored by psychologists. Another solution frequently adopted by small schools is for the health office, or for the counseling service, or both, to employ a psychiatrist not as a regular member of the staff but as a consultant, called upon either regularly or according to need.

Brandeis University started organizing a psychological counseling service when the school was in its fifth year of existence, with a student body of 740, and with the administrative structure still minimal and plastic; there were no set traditions to function as immovable obstacles to novel enterprises. Consequently it was possible in organizing and developing the service to proceed in an exploratory, experimental fashion, taking into account the experiences of other schools without having to imitate their example. The usual conflicts and pressures were of course not lacking, and, in dealing with them, strategic mistakes were occasionally made; there were times, in fact, when the continued existence of the service was endangered. Yet, in time, the crucial issues proved capable of resolution and, with the help of

[2] Farnsworth, D. L. and Munter, P. K. "The Role of the College Psychiatrist." In Blaine, G. B. and McArthur, Ch. C. (eds.), *Emotional Problems of the Students.* New York: Appleton-Century-Crofts, 1961.

Organization of a Counseling Service

many people, more adequate and mutually acceptable arrangements were gradually worked out. The major organizational landmarks in the service's evolution to its present status were the following:

1. 1952. Establishment of a psychological counseling service was recommended and initiated by the chairman of the Psychology Department who nominated the present writer for the position of director, with simultaneous appointment to the faculty. The policy was formulated that the Counseling Center was to be an independent administrative unit, with a separate budget and a separate location on campus, and that its files would not be accessible to any other office. Agreements were made with the Office of Student Personnel and with the Health Office about the distribution of work and about certain preconditions of counseling.

2. 1953. A policy was formulated about employing as counselors only clinically well-trained personnel and money was provided for hiring a doctoral psychologist as the second, full-time staff member. Money was provided in the budget for employing a psychiatrist as a consultant to the Center on a regular basis, with the view of utilizing his services for supervisory work with the Center's counselors.

3. 1954. Appointment of a Visiting Committee to the Center, composed of the Psychiatric Consultant and two other distinguished psychiatrists active in the field of education, was made; the Committee meets with the Center's staff yearly to hear the Director's report and to discuss current problems. At the first meeting, some of the rules governing the Center's interaction with other offices were modified, with the Committee's support, in order to meet more fully the requirement of confidentiality.

4. 1959. Appointment of a psychiatrist to the staff of the school's Health Office was made, substituting for the former ar-

rangement of calling local psychiatrists as consultants according to need. The College Psychiatrist, who spends one day weekly on campus, in functioning as a liaison between the Health Office and the Center, helped to work out effective methods of insuring proper attention to the medical aspect of the students' problems.

5. 1960. The Center's continued close connection with the Department of Psychology was formalized through transfer of the service from the general jurisdiction of an administrative dean (Dean of Students) to that of the Academic Dean (when the position of the Dean of Students had been created five years earlier, the Counseling Center was automatically placed under him). This move enabled the Center to get full benefit from its academic connection. At present all those members of the counseling staff who meet the Department's academic standards, and who work at the school full time, can be given full faculty status, regardless of whether they actually teach some courses or devote all of their time to counseling. With this administrative change the present organizational structure of the Center was completed.

It might be useful to complement this enumeration of the main steps in the progressive development of the Center's structure by a discussion of the main false moves — policies and practices that have been tried out and proved not to work, or to work to the detriment of our task. In some instances the poor effects were foreseen, but no better solutions seemed available at the time.

In starting the Center it proved necessary to agree to notify the Director of Student Personnel of the names of the students who were seen in prolonged counseling; he saw this as the only way to insure the possibility of consultation in cases of those counseled students who might get into disciplinary or academic troubles. The students, however, though they saw the validity of the motive, never accepted the rule; not one of the open

Organization of a Counseling Service

meetings held by the Center's staff with the students passed without vigorous objections being raised against it; in fact we had reasons to suspect that some students cut short their contact with the Center in order to qualify as non-reportable "brief consultation" cases. Eventually it proved feasible to take care of the problem by different means. It was arranged that the agenda of the Administrative Committee (which makes all major decisions concerning individual students) would be sent to the Center in advance of its meetings; this would enable the counselor to take initiative in speaking on behalf of his counselee, if he should feel that the student's mental balance, or his progress in therapy, would be seriously endangered by the proposed administrative measure. Actually, the school's dealing with the students being usually reasonable and lenient, such cases hardly ever occurred. In the exceptional instances of the Center's interaction with the Administration it is understood that the counselor is free to give the student concerned an exact account of the part he himself has played in it, in order to avoid misperception and confusion.

In the matter of insuring attention to the medical aspects of the students' problems the initially adopted method was that of requiring each student who came for prolonged counseling to have a general physical check-up at the Health Office. This method, which (like the reporting of names) involved all students in order to meet the needs of a few, proved cumbersome and ineffective. It was a waste of time both for the medical staff and for the students who often managed to avoid the check-up through procrastination. This measure could have greatly delayed the acceptance of counseling by the students were it not for the saving grace of the "prolonged counseling" clause. It was agreed from the start that in case of students who had no physical complaints the request would be made only if the student, after 4–5 sessions, decided to continue in counseling; this gave him a chance to become involved to the point where, for the sake of continuing, he would agree to go through the routine. An insistence on a medical check-up as a preliminary to the very initiation of counseling might have effectively kept away the majority of the students who actually approached the Center. The advent of a psychiatrist to the Health Office enabled us to solve the issue of a medical check-up in a rational and effective way.

At one point, before a psychiatrist was appointed, we tried to improve our communication with the Health Office by sharing with them the services of the Center's Psychiatric Consultant. This plan did not work, because the services required by the two offices are very different, and one person is not likely to provide both. The Consultant of the Center shares with the Director the responsibility for maintaining the therapeutic work of the staff on a high level of competence by providing consultation on difficult cases, but mainly by doing regular supervisory work with the junior staff members. (Although the senior staff members also take part in training new counselors, this job can be done much more effectively by one who is outside the Center's and the school's structure and not the counselor's administrative superior.) The Consultant, a senior member of his profession, with experience in supervisory work, has his time filled with the positions he holds or with private practice; he will see the counselors in regular weekly sessions in his office but he will not ordinarily be able and willing to come out to the campus to handle emergencies, to hold office hours, or to have extensive talks with the members of the administration. To insure such services the school must employ competent younger psychiatrists, and employ them on a regular basis. It is essential to make these different functions clear to the administration; otherwise it will appear natural and economical to attempt to combine them in one person.

Other examples of arrangements that work, or do not work,

in a setting of a small college will be found throughout other chapters. The reader is referred particularly to the chapter written by our first College Psychiatrist who stayed with the school for two years; to him fell the major part of the difficult task of establishing policies and practices of working with those students in whose handling the school administration is also involved.

An issue that does not exactly fall into the category of "false moves" is that of the Counseling Center's involvement in psychological testing. During the first years of its existence the Center sponsored a modest program of psychological testing of Freshmen previously initiated by the school; each entering class was given the group Rorschach and a Sentence Completion Test specially adapted for this age group. However, while we felt that the test data might be potentially useful, we had to discourage the Administration's hope that they could serve to provide a list of students who were likely to become disturbed in college; such listing was supposed to prevent future trouble, possibly by alerting someone on the campus about those to be watched or handled in a special way. In this instance, as so often, the psychologists were more skeptical of the predictive power of isolated tests than were, wishfully, the administrators; we doubted the wisdom of informing, e.g., the graduate students who served as dormitory counselors that some of their charges had "suicidal indices" on the Rorschach. Furthermore, for any sort of a half-credible performance of spotting the potentially disturbed among the 200 new students an inordinate amount of time would be used up in working on records, time which we felt was more profitably spent in talking to the students themselves. We did attempt, for one Freshman class, to identify by quick impressionistic Rorschach evidence the potentially disturbed students and to check against this list the names of those who subsequently applied for counseling. The fact that the correlation between the two lists proved negligible can be variously interpreted, but it served to confirm our growing conviction that the testing program was of little usefulness to the school.

To have the test data on file proved helpful in the case of some of the students seen at the Center. The counselors were able to draw on them for additional insights in some difficult cases, and could occasionally use them for a stimulating discussion with the student himself. In one instance the Sentence Completion Test provided the means of opening up with a student the concealed issue of his recent suicidal attempts: the counselor had been informed of them, in confidence, by the student's friend and found them clearly spelled out in his test responses. Lastly, for some hesitant students, an inquiry about their test results served as a covert mode of approach to the Center. Yet all these occasions for making use of the test data were infrequent from the start and became increasingly rare as the counselors acquired experience with the range of problems and disturbances encountered among students. When the Student Personnel Office arrived at the decision to discontinue the testing program of which the psychological tests were a part we had no strong reason to oppose this decision.

Clinical tests are essentially a short-cut to diagnosis, useful for questions of disposition. When ample time is available for continued interviews we encounter very few cases in which testing appears to be of essence. In such cases arrangements for it can easily be made off-campus, with individuals or agencies that specialize in this work. The same is true of vocational testing. In a small school the advantages of offering a testing service on campus are offset by complications that arise when the counselor is also a tester. It seems to be generally true that the existence of such service is more often an invitation to the school administrators and outside agencies to seek information about students than it is of help to the students themselves. Those few students who only seek to find out their "test results," without being

Organization of a Counseling Service

willing to discuss the concerns that motivate them, are not likely to benefit from whatever information the psychologist finds possible to impart in this limiting setting. The use of tests in the service of research and of clinical teaching is of course an issue quite separate from the question of their usefulness in a student-oriented counseling program.

A word is perhaps in place about the factors that help a counseling service to establish conditions necessary for its survival and growth. The first and foremost of course is the ability to render competent therapeutic service to students; after its value has become apparent to many, a strong student opinion will be a definite factor in the service's evolution. Yet, in a circular fashion, this factor cannot come into being as long as not enough students come, or as long as they are not given enough time when they come.

In working out arrangements with the administration there is no substitute for bringing disagreements into the open, experimenting, comparing notes, and learning from shared experiences; there are definite limits, however, on this exploratory, flexible, person-oriented approach. If certain basic principles — that of safeguarding confidentiality, for example — are not established from the start, chances of introducing them later may prove very poor. Consequently it is essential for the success of the task that the person charged with the establishment of the service have some sources of prestige and support both inside and outside the school. The support of a strong department, high academic rank, or high standing in one's profession, can help one through the difficulties of the initial period; readiness to resign if conditions essential for effective work are not granted is a definite asset. Second, it is always useful to put the administrative officers in touch with some sources of modern professional opinion on the debated issues; in our case this has been one of the functions admirably fulfilled by the Visiting Committee to whose meetings guests from other departments were often invited. When a dean realizes that any professional worker who is worth his salt will make the identical demands the battle has been half won; it is fully won only when the empirical reasons for these demands have become obvious and arrangements have been worked out that are genuinely acceptable to all.

Even then, there remains the problem of stabilizing and safeguarding these achievements. In a small school with a limited number of administrative positions, a change of key personnel may undo what has been achieved and may necessitate a repetition of the whole laborious process. To insure the continuity of the arrangements that have proved workable it is useful to formulate them in writing with the agreement of all concerned, and with the explicit understanding that they can be changed only for substantial reasons and after thorough discussion. It is also essential to have these policies open to the students' inspection and for the staff to be able to answer clearly and unequivocally any questions the students may ask.

The following excerpt from the description of the Brandeis Counseling Center in the Student Handbook for 1961–62 incorporates some of our policies and shows how the Center defines its functions to the students.[3]

> The Psychological Counseling Center is an adjunct of the Department of Psychology. It provides, without charge, the services of trained and experienced clinical psychologists to all students desiring help in the solution of emotional problems, and in removing inner obstacles to optimal personal growth. The student can bring to the counselor any problem that troubles him or her, whether it is fear of examinations, difficulties in studying, conflicts with family or friends, boy-

---

[3] The reader is also referred to the informational booklet "Some Questions and Answers About Psychological Counseling" which is reprinted in the appendix.

girl problems, uncertainty about one's choice of vocation, general self-doubt, depressive moods, or just vague feelings of dissatisfaction and tension. Such problems and disturbances are a common occurrence among college students. They are in no way "abnormal," but they need not be accepted as unavoidable. They can usually be helped by increased self-awareness and self-knowledge, and this is what counseling aims to achieve. The counselors do not give advice or propose solutions; the student himself, by talking out his or her feelings and exploring problems with the counselor, discovers their interconnections and reasons and is enabled to find the solutions that are best for him. Contrary to the uninformed view that making use of psychological counseling is a sign of weakness, the Center views its services as adjunctive to the overall educational enterprise. The primary aim of counseling is the development of the student's own initiative and independent thinking.

As the student must feel free to talk about all personal matters, full confidentiality is a necessary condition of psychological counseling; safeguarding it is a major concern of the Center. After years of experimentation, the Center has worked out the following policies in order to insure confidentiality: Students can contact the Center directly, without any intermediaries. All referrals to the Center are on a voluntary basis. The students' communications are held in strict professional confidence, and so are the names of the students counseled. If a situation arises requiring communication with the parents, Health Office, or Student Personnel, this is discussed with the student. This rule may be waived only in rare instances of serious emergency that require quick action, e.g., an impending major breakdown.

If any member of the college community wishes help in finding the best way to handle the problem of a student about whom he is concerned, we provide an informal consultation, but without disclosing whether or not the student discussed is known to the staff or the Center. If an outside agency — the family doctor, a psychiatrist, a clinic — requests information about a student who is or has been in counseling, the Center asks the agency to provide a "permission for release of information" signed by the student.

Regular appointments can usually be offered to a student as soon as he contacts the Center, but it is best to do so early in the year. Those who enter counseling in the fall can be provided with weekly counseling sessions during the whole academic year. The limits on the extent of our services are subject to change depending on the size of the staff in relation to the size of the student body, and on the extent of the demand for counseling. If the student after a period of counseling wishes to continue work started at the Center we are prepared to help him or her make arrangements with an off-campus clinic or psychotherapist. The same service is offered those students whose situation makes college counseling appear inadvisable or insufficient. The Center does not provide psychological or vocational testing, but we can help students to make arrangements for testing.

The organizational evolution of the Center has been accompanied by a slow but steady growth of the counseling facilities and of their utilization by the students. The absolute number of students seen during the school year has almost tripled over ten years and the percentage of attendance has doubled: in 1961–62 16% of the total undergraduate student body were seen at the Center, as compared with 8% in 1952–53. Adding to the 197 undergraduates who were counseled last year the 24 students who were seen only by the College Psychiatrist and not by the Center raises the percent to 18. This is a very high figure for a college counseling service of our type. The Congdon-Lothrop survey gives 2.5% as the median for those (32) school offices which provide therapeutic services exclusively; percentages higher than ten are rarely quoted. In the last years we have also extended our service to include a limited amount of help to graduate students. During the last school year 12 of these were seen at the Center and 9 more by the College Psychiatrist — altogether about 6.5% of the graduates who were in residence during the year.

To evaluate these numbers as indicators of the students' acceptance of the counseling service it must be borne in mind that from the start we accepted none but purely voluntary referrals, consistently refusing the semi-forced ones occasionally attempted by the administration. We were acutely aware of the fact that a student who is advised to go to the Center by a person in authority may not feel free to reject this advice. The staff of the Student Personnel Office quickly learned to make referrals only in the form of very tentative suggestions and *not* to check on their results either with the student or with the Center. This manner of referral clearly implies that the decision about counseling is the students', that the service is for them alone, and encourages them to approach it on their own. Actually, from the second year of the Center's existence the large majority of the students have been self-referred, the percentage varying from 70 to 90 in different years. In a certain proportion of these self-referral cases the student's friends participate in referral, either by making the original suggestion, or by supporting his own tentative plan. In the year 1961–62, for example, 58% of the students said in applying for counseling that the decision was entirely their own, 12% credited their friends with the suggestion, and 12% gave equal weight to their own motive and to the support of a friend. These proportions are typical of many years. The variability in the percentage of total self-referrals is due less to changes in students' attitudes than to the varying activity of the referring agencies of the school. Thus, a year after a psychiatrist joined the staff of the Health Office referrals through this office increased from practically zero to 8% of the total. Referrals through the Office of Student Personnel, through the dormitory counselors, and through the faculty have varied from year to year, depending on policies, personnel, and on the special efforts periodically made by the Center to acquaint a given group with its work. Referrals made through any one of the school channels, however, rarely exceeded 10% of the totals; combined, they never exceeded 30%. Referrals through the students' families and outside agencies have been minimal. Among the faculty, members of the Department of Psychology, including graduate students, have been the most active in referrals. This is particularly true of those teachers who were also counselors on the staff of the Center. The function served by certain specially taught courses in getting the students interested in counseling will be described in detail in the chapter by Dr. Jones.

The average length of the counseling periods, which in the first year of our work equalled four sessions, has grown steadily; in the last four years it varied between 10 and 12 hours. This increase is a combined function of the wish for more extensive work shared alike by the students and the counselors and of the gradual increase of the staff which has permitted a partial meeting of this wish. In 1961–62 the staff of the Center provided the time equivalent to that of four full-time counselors for a student body of 1270 undergraduates and 364 graduates. During the first years of the Center's existence only one third of our contacts exceeded four sessions; the limitation in the rest of the cases was usually not by the students' choice. In the last four years the proportion of students who were seen for more than four sessions varied between 55% and 65% of the total; from 25% to 30% were seen for more than 15 sessions, and no student who wished to make maximal use of the service was barred from it for extraneous reasons. The present time limit of one academic year (or 7–8 months of weekly sessions) allows the student a maximum of about 30 counseling hours; this number can be exceeded when an increase seems imperative or highly desirable. By comparison with the majority of schools on which relevant data are available this is a very liberal allowance of time. The most frequently quoted averages of the number of sessions per student vary between 4 and 6, which is about one half of the averages we had in the last four years. Even with this allowance, however, we cannot expect to meet the needs of all students; we encourage those who need prolonged treatment and can meet the expense to transfer to private therapists as soon as they are ready for this move. On the average 25% of the students seen at the Center each year accept the idea of continuing therapy outside the school; the majority of them eventually act on this decision. There are many others who would benefit greatly from an extended period of therapy, but who for various reasons cannot arrange for it; an extension of college counseling to a two-year period would solve the problem of most of them. We estimate that with our present arrangements the current needs of about 50% of the students who apply for counseling can be adequately met by the Center itself.

We have made some attempts to collect data on the differential rates of the utilization of the counseling service by different categories of students. The obvious categories are the four classes, the sexes, the academically successful and the failing, and those majoring in different academic fields. Some of these data have been collected systematically through the years, while others are based on spot-checks and would have to be amplified and verified to be more than merely suggestive.

The demands made on the counseling service by each of the four classes have varied within a fairly narrow range and apparently randomly. The only observable slight trend, and one going contrary to what one might expect, is the less than average participation of Freshmen: in 5 years out of 8 for which these figures were computed a smaller percent of Freshmen than of any of the other classes applied for counseling, the difference being of the order of 7%–10% versus 11%–15%. Although in each school year college entrance precipitates acute emotional reactions in a few students, it seems that the majority of Freshmen anticipate initial adjustment difficulties and struggle with them on their own, hoping that the next year will be happier. This interpretation is supported by the fact that the percentage of Freshmen seeking counseling caught up with that of other classes after the Office of Student Personnel made a special effort to spot and refer the disturbed among the new students. A detailed description of the counseling service in the Student Handbook may have also contributed to this recent change.

For one of the recent years (1960–61) we have computed the percentage of students in counseling in terms of their levels of academic performance; 44% of the students counseled during that year reported good or excellent grades (A's and B's); 38% had fair grades (B− or C+ averages); 18% had poor grades, although only the minority in this group were in actual danger of failing.[4] These figures bear out our general impression that the counseling service, far from being exclusively the refuge of the failing, is being used widely by the gifted, promising students. This impression is also indirectly confirmed by the fact that difficulties in studying, of different degrees of severity, are not the most prominent category of complaints the students bring to the Center. Such complaints increase during the years which follow the tightening of academic standards and demands, but even during the year most marked by this concern only 25% of all counseled students presented difficulties in studying as their main initial complaint; in most years this percentage has been

---

[4] The distribution of grades of students who graduated in 1962 puts 34% in the A and B group, 60% in the C+ and B− group, 6% in the C group. In terms of the total student population this is a selected group since the failing and many of the poor students do not reach graduation.

close to 15, although the picture, as we shall see later, is not identical for the two sexes.

The degree of participation in counseling of students majoring in different fields was computed for those members of the class of 1962 who actually graduated from Brandeis, omitting all those who in the course of the four years had dropped out for various reasons. Students graduating in the School of Humanities showed the lowest degree of participation in counseling: 20% of them were seen at the Center in the course of four years. The corresponding percentage for the School of Science was 23, for the School of Creative Arts 24, for the School of Social Science 27. The high percent in the last case is due largely to the high participation in counseling of psychology majors (the largest major in the school) which amounted to 30%; the percent for the students majoring in the other combined social science fields was 25. For the rest of the specific subjects within the four fields the comparison is not informative because of the small numbers involved. It may be of interest, however, to note that the only (small) major that equalled psychology (with 30%) was philosophy, and the only one that exceeded it (with 50%) was theatre arts, another small major. Essentially, the review of the single majors in conjunction with the data on the schools indicates that participation in counseling is not a concern of any one special group, but is distributed over the total range of school subjects.

By far the most pronounced and consistent differences in the utilization of the Center have been observed between the sexes. In the first five years of the Center's existence the percent of male students making use of it never exceeded 9, while that of the females varied between 12 and 14. In the following 3 years the difference in the participation of the two sexes was greatly reduced, but recently it reappeared: in 1961–62, 19% of the undergraduate girls and 12% of the undergraduate boys applied for counseling help. In the past girls also provided a higher percentage of self-referrals and had longer periods of counseling; in 1958–59, for example, the average number of counseling sessions was 10 for the boys, 13 for the girls. Both of these trends have been reduced with time, but are still quite prominent. Initially there was also a trend for a greater acceptance by the girls of referrals to outside therapists, but in the last years this difference has tended to disappear.

The greater utilization of the Counseling Service by the girls might lead one to believe that the incidence of disturbance must be higher among them than among the boys — at least within our particular population. Although this hypothesis can neither be proven nor disproven without a special study, some relevant data contradict this assumption and suggest a different explanation.

As part of the Center's routine all students, after a few sessions, are rated by the counselor as to the degree of their disturbance on a three point scale: disturbance slight, moderate, serious. Under "disturbance slight" we list essentially healthy students who come because of some situationally caused upset, or of some difficulty inherent in the process of normal adolescent development. These cases comprise an average of 20% of all those who come, but it may be safely assumed that the majority of students with problems of that order of magnitude never show up at the Center. "Disturbance moderate" is noted for those in whom the difficulties of adolescence are much more pronounced than is usual and for those who show some chronic neurotic patterns that are not excessively handicapping. This is the largest group, comprising close to 70% of all students who come to the Center. The first and the second groups taken together fall well within the limits of what is generally assumed to be "normal" with regard to their personality organization; they comprise about 90% of our group. The remaining 10% are made up of severely neurotic or extremely immature adolescents who function after a fashion, in spite of their handicap;

Organization of a Counseling Service

occasionally encountered cases of pre-psychotic or psychopathic personalities also belong in this group.

When the distribution of ratings is made separately for the two sexes the boys appear to be markedly worse off than the girls. In most years a smaller percent of boys than girls are rated as only slightly disturbed and in all years a higher percent is rated as seriously disturbed; sometimes the percent of the boys given this rating is double that of the girls. Taking this finding in conjunction with the lower rate of the boys' participation in counseling, it seems plausible to assume that the boys prefer to struggle on their own until the difficulties become unmanageable, or until a girl friend induces the student to give "psychology" a try. Actually such attitudes are frequently expressed by the boys. The passive connotations of the idea of seeking help are much less acceptable to them than they are to the girls.

Further light is thrown on the issue by a review of sex differences in the distribution of the "main initial complaints," i.e. of the manifest troubles that bring students to the Center. The largest category of complaints for the total group pertains to difficulties in interpersonal relations, be it relations with age-equals, with parents, or with the opposite sex. This is the chief complaint in c. 45% of all cases, the figure varying between 35% and 55% in different years. In most years, however, the girls' complaints are centered around interpersonal issues much more frequently than those of the boys, the difference being sometimes of the order of 20%. On the other hand, in the category of "difficulties in studying" the boys quite regularly exceed the girls, the difference being quite pronounced: the proportion of those who present this as their main complaint has varied between 17% and 34% for the boys, between 8% and 19% for the girls. This difference is paralleled by the difference in the distribution of grades of the counseled male and female students: almost 50% of the girls counseled in

1960–61, as compared with 35% of the boys, were receiving A's and B's, while 13% of the girls and 25% of the boys had poor or failing grades. The two other major categories of complaints — those related to the adolescent's search for personal identity and values, and complaints about depressive moods or other specific symptoms — showed no consistent differences between the two sexes.

Regardless of the underlying causes of the differences in the complaints, they probably play a role in the difference of the two sexes' attitudes towards counseling. While a considerable proportion of boys still seems to view counseling as the last resort, to be tried only if troubles mount or if failure threatens, many girls welcome the opportunity to work out personal problems even if they do not represent a major or an immediate threat. Thus they make good pioneers in the large scale, preventive utilization of an early opportunity for developing insight and self-knowledge which college counseling should aim to provide. If our experiences at Brandeis have any general validity, women's colleges, and to a lesser extent coeducational schools, should have much less difficulty than men's colleges in establishing a counseling program that would be widely accepted and spontaneously utilized by the students.

II

ESTABLISHING A PSYCHIATRIC SERVICE IN A COLLEGE

Leo Kovar

We believe that certain fairly typical problems arise during the establishment of a psychiatric service in a university setting. Although what will be described is the particular experience at Brandeis University, some of the dilemmas which had to be faced as a policy was being worked out — with errors made and corrected along the way — are probably shared by all university psychiatric services. We shall omit the description of the psychiatrist's day-to-day functioning in the college setting and shall focus on the issues which arise in establishing a policy during the initial period of service, and on the solutions which were eventually found in this particular school. To anticipate our major conclusions: our experiences clearly indicate that the psychiatrist's policies in relation to students and the administration should be unequivocal and public.

The particular situation which motivates an institution to enlist a new service points implicitly to the institution's general expectations from that service, both in regard to its nature and scope. Inevitably there will be conflict between those expectations and the practices held to be appropriate by those providing the new service. When the role of a new service is clearly defined by tradition and does not overlap significantly that of another service within the institution, there is likely to be a minimum of conflict; there is then less need to establish clear policies which spell out publicly the specific functions and specific limitations of function of that service. Such is the case for a traditional, i.e., non-psychiatric, medical department in a university. A psychiatric service in a university, however, is necessarily in the middle of many intra-institutional conflicts of interests. Some arise inevitably as part of the structure and function of the school; others are avoidable and arise largely from unrealistic expectations on the part of the institution, or from personal prejudice or vested interest on the part of the personnel. We shall describe here the general situation which prompted the school to recruit a psychiatric service, some of the conflicting points of view which emerged in connection with the overlapping of functions, and the trials and errors of working out a tenable policy structure which would reconcile the demands of clinical work with the requirements of the various departments concerned.

The University in 1959 invited a psychiatrist to join the Medical Department on a part-time basis. At this point in the history of the school the Counseling Center, staffed by clinical psychologists, had been in existence for seven years. During these years the Center employed the regular services of a psychiatric consultant who met with the staff members off-campus in a supervisory capacity; he had, however, no close connection with the Medical Department and was not easily accessible to the school Administration. Within the Medical Department a psychiatrist from the neighboring community had been retained as consultant for emergencies and for occasional evaluations of student problems with administrative implications. The shortcomings of this arrangement had become increasingly apparent. The Medical Department would not ordinarily call in the consultant for "routine" or non-emergency evaluations and consequently many students seen by the physicians for minor psychosomatic complaints, or occasionally for overt psychiatric complaints, went without special psychological attention. In such situations, often because of a general reluctance to make referrals to a non-medical facility, physicians on the medical staff did not make sufficient use of the Counseling Center. The common biases of non-psychiatric physicians were present in varying degree; they were against "too much psychologizing" for fear the "real problems" would be obscured, and they were embroiled in the traditional debate over the degree of status and responsibility to be accorded clinical psychologists. In this regard, even when students had been referred to outside therapists by the Center, the Medical Department felt that this fact, and the name of the therapist, should be on its records in case of emergency.

On the other side, there was of course a good deal of resentment felt by the Counseling Center toward the Medical Department, primarily because of the Medical Department's attitudes, but also because of cumbersome regulations which had been instituted as safeguards against the possible disregard of physical factors. Each student seen more than four times at the Counseling Center was required to have a routine physical examination by the Medical Department. Despite the acknowledged archaic nature of diagnosis by default, the implication here was strong that psychiatric diagnosis should be made only after and by exclusion of "medical" illness. The requirement of a routine physical examination for every student in prolonged counseling also effectively negated the confidentiality of the psychotherapeutic relationship, a requirement to which the medical people, fairly typically, at best paid only lip service. The Center was thus put in the awkward position of having to direct its counselees to follow a procedure which it felt was opposed to good therapeutic practice. Many students who "illegally" circumvented the requirement probably received tacit moral support from their counselors and for some this meant using neurotic avoidance devices identical with their very pressing pathology.

Thus, what should normally have been a congenial and constructive relationship of mutual referral and consultation between a Counseling Center and a Medical Department had become one of mutual distrust and guardedness, with students inevitably caught in the middle. One is reminded, on a more drastic scale, of the description of increased disturbance of patients on a mental hospital ward as a function of conflict between staff members, as described in *The Mental Hospital* by Stanton and Schwartz.[1]

The second major source of dissatisfaction was really a corollary of the first. As must happen in the course of any clinical practice, disturbed or anti-social behavior developed at times unexpectedly and at times was temporarily uncontrollable. When such occurrences came to the attention of the Administration, the Director of the Counseling Center was promptly sought out to determine whether the student was known to the Center. The stated reason for the request was to gain all relevant information which might be of help in aiding the student. Usually it developed that two major anxieties were being expressed. First, the Administration was understandably concerned about the occurrence of destructive or grossly bizarre behavior, both from the standpoint of the welfare of the students involved and from the standpoint of the school's public image. Second, someone or something had to be held responsible for allowing a student's state of emotional disturbance to reach such proportions, so that repetitions might be avoided. This wish was understandable, but it was being expressed without regard for the possibility of its real fulfillment. The thought was not seriously entertained that in any student body a certain number of acute severe disturbances was inevitable and that no therapeutic agency, no matter how effective, could serve as an absolute preventative. Rather, thinking became somewhat magical at such crises and it was usually assumed, tacitly or openly, that if only "someone" had been informed "in

---

[1] Stanton, Alfred H., and Schwartz, Morris S. *The Mental Hospital; a Study of Institutional Participation in Psychiatric Illness and Treatment.* New York: Basic Books, Inc., 1954.

time" the disturbance could have been prevented. "Someone" generally meant either the Administration itself, which would have stepped in as disciplinarian, or a psychiatrist who with superior wisdom would have managed a problem which retrospectively and because of "failure" was assumed to have been "mismanaged" by the psychologist. "In time" really implied the wish for reinstatement of a routine submission of names of all students consulting the Center.

This, then, was the general climate of attitudes and conflicts involving the Administration, the Medical Department, and the Counseling Center which had evolved over several years and which led the Dean of Students to the conviction that a staff psychiatrist should be added to the Medical Department. This decision was also facilitated by the fact that the Administration was aware of the growing acceptance of psychiatric services by the leading schools of the country. The decision was not opposed from any quarter. At an earlier period, before the relative administrative autonomy of the Counseling Center had been fully accepted, its staff would have had misgivings about this step as a possible move toward the incorporation of the Center into the structure of the Medical Department; by this time, however, such misgivings had been dispelled. The psychiatrist was cordially welcomed by everybody concerned.

The expectations each agency had of the psychiatrist were of course different. The Administration hoped that the psychiatrist would serve first as an institutional safeguard against students developing unexpected breakdowns and second as a watchdog over the Counseling Center. Despite the fact that the Director of the Counseling Center was held in very high esteem personally and the work of the Center was regarded as of high calibre, there remained some general uneasiness about professional standards, with the usual spectre of the grossly mismanaged case offered as justification for closer supervision by the Administration. The Counseling Center hoped that the psychiatrist would assume the management of borderline and psychotic students, would satisfy, as far as feasible, the Administration's desire for consultation concerning cases requiring disciplinary action, and would rectify the relationship between itself and the Medical Department. Finally, the Medical Department, whose expectations were probably least, seemed to welcome the psychiatrist primarily as someone to whom referrals could be made, thus bypassing its own reluctance to refer to a non-medical facility. If the psychiatrist in turn wished to refer students to the Counseling Center after his own evaluation, that was his business and his responsibility. Clearly, the psychiatrist, on the campus one day a week, could handle therapeutically only a small fraction of the referrals which should emanate from the other physicians.

The general problems seemed to resemble somewhat those faced by a new department of psychiatry in a general hospital, first with respect to other medical departments, second with respect to the hospital administration. In the setting of a general hospital psychiatry is the specialty physicians are likely to be least knowledgeable about. Very often the attitude toward a new department of psychiatry is likely to be determined mainly by the staff's need to refer unmanageable, or unresponsive, or undiagnosable patients rather than by any primary interest in the subject of psychiatry itself. The administration of a general hospital, not unlike the administration of a university, is apt to be overly preoccupied with the nuisance aspect of psychiatric problems because the face of the institution must be kept clean. Thus, despite an enlightened view of psychiatric illness the administration may insist on unnecessary mechanical safeguards which tend to stifle the efficient practice of good psychiatry. A common situation encountered in many general hospitals is an irrational reluctance to admit mildly disturbed psychiatric patients to a non-psychiatric ward. The occasional unpleasant behavior of psychiatric patients in a general medical hospital ward is viewed with much less tolerance than are aesthetically disturbing manifestations of physical illness.

The most easily resolved aspect of the situation the psychiatrist was faced with in the college was the formal relationship between the Medical Department and the Counseling Center. The Medical Department, composed entirely of part-time physicians practicing medicine and surgery in the community, was more than willing to relinquish all psychiatric responsibility. Although the degree of interest and sophistication in the subject varied considerably, no one of the physicians had time available to pursue with any significant interest the psychiatric aspect of student life. The head of the department was occasionally asked to pass on the admission to the University of a student with known past psychiatric illness and was pleased to be able to relinquish this task.

The staff of the Counseling Center welcomed the psychiatrist as someone congenial to their point of view, who believed that well-trained psychologists were qualified to do psychotherapy, and who could represent their point of view authoritatively to the Medical Department. It was thus a simple matter to set up weekly meetings with the staff of the Center in which all cases with any possible medical aspect were presented. The psychiatrist then used his own judgment in making recommendations for medical referral, eliminating the cumbersome and ineffectual routine physical examination and virtually restoring the original degree of confidentiality for the student. The content of these meetings gradually expanded into a complete and free interchange of professional information and served as the focus for working out solutions to the remaining professional-administrative policy problem.

The elaboration of the psychiatrist's role in relation to the Administration proved to be more difficult. The presence of a dean who was psychologically aware and personally dedicated to the emotional well-being of the student body made the task both easier and harder. On a formal level the psychiatrist was virtually given *carte blanche* to work out the most efficacious policy for himself. Informally, however, the good personal rapport and the agreement about professional goals made it awkward to be "sticky" about refusing to share what often seemed like "harmless" information which could be used to the student's benefit. For example, a student who was reported for cheating on an examination divulged voluntarily to the Dean that he had been consulting the university psychiatrist for unrelated problems. The Dean, wishing to act as constructively as possible, felt that he needed some psychiatric justification for recommending relative leniency to the administrative committee. He asked the psychiatrist "in confidence" if he could provide information from his knowledge of the boy which could be used to support the recommendation that the cheating be regarded as a symptomatic act amenable to therapy, rather than as an offense calling for strong disciplinary action. The Dean was persuaded that he could make his point at least as well from his own firsthand knowledge of the boy and from his own conviction of what was administratively proper. The essential policy problem became crystallized, as often happens, through such exceptional cases.

When a student faced impending administrative action, either disciplining for anti-social behavior or severance for academic failure, the established procedure had been to deal with the student's behavior as such on the basis more or less of "just deserts." The Dean himself was not content to deal with such crises in the lives of students in a perfunctory fashion and generally devoted much effort to exploring with the student the underlying difficulties which had led to his impasse. However, the Dean, though sensitive and knowledgeable, felt he was not equipped to help the student assess maximally the factors contributing to his predicament. He would often consult the Director of the Counseling Center informally, presenting the problem under consideration with the hope that some fresh professional insight could be offered. At times a direct request would be made for advice on management. The Director of the Counseling Center would of course demur since the integrity of her Department depended on strict separation of therapeutic and administrative roles; to be effective the separation had to be extended to students never seen at the Center, for obvious reasons. First, any distinction made between students who had been seen and students who had not been seen would effectively be breaking confidentiality. Second, the image of the Director as someone who might intercede with the Administration, either benevolently or punitively, would certainly be out of keeping with the requirements of a clinical service on the campus. Thus, comments or suggestions had to be made in the most general terms, reminding the Dean constantly that the handling of any particular student problem must be based on his own judgment.

The Dean, while unable to disagree logically with the position of the Director, nevertheless felt that a chronic vacuum existed by not having a professional psychological adviser and confidante. When the psychiatrist arrived he was viewed by the Dean as a natural choice for this role. He could be in intimate touch with individual student problems and also with the general institutional context and yet not find it necessary to preserve for himself as pure a therapeutic role as did the Counseling Center. The Counseling Center, after all, had formulated its function in educational as well as therapeutic terms and accordingly viewed itself as an integral component of the University's teaching structure. As a part of the educational context of the University its function was to teach, to be sure in the special sense of self-knowledge and with the distinction that the reward to the student was entirely internal, with no A's for successful psychotherapy; but as such it had to preserve its role as mentor and divorce itself from all aspects of the University which had to do with the management of community life or with external academic achievement. The psychiatrist, it was hoped, would be primarily identified with the Medical Service, and as part of an ancillary department could properly be a consultant to the Administration on just those matters from which the Counseling Center had declared itself immune.

As one might expect, one of the most common complaints which students presented to the psychiatrist was a concern with poor study habits or failing grades. Many unfortunately awaited the development of a pre-examination crisis or actual scholastic failure before seeking assistance. Some reached the psychiatrist only when academic severance was pending; they were usually referred by the Dean near the time of departure from the school. It was with this last group that the essential problem emerged. A common procedure that had been followed was to grant a student a year's leave of absence, following which he could apply for reinstatement on the basis of demonstrated change in his academic performance pattern; this usually entailed part-time enrollment at another school, often in combination with a regular part-time job. Psychotherapy during the period of leave was encouraged by the Dean and usually a recommendation was solicited from the therapist when the student applied for reinstatement. Rarely, of course, would a therapist reveal negative indications for his patient's returning to school, so that these communications added little of value. The hope was expressed that perhaps the outside therapists would feel freer to communicate the whole truth to the college psychiatrist than to the Administration and that the psychiatrist, without divulging details, could pass on general recommendations to the Administration. In effect, such a procedure would amount to passing the buck to the therapist and would require him to make a recommendation without divulging this to his patient; this approach was discouraged as both unethical and impractical.

The psychiatrist, however, still shared with the Administration the feeling that even if some students unfortunately remained oblivious of their inner difficulties until the emergence of a crisis, at least more might be learned from the misfortune itself and more effective use might be made of the period of leave. Students who dropped out because of performance grossly below their capabilities — and these comprised the bulk of academic drop-outs — were most commonly youngsters with obsessive character traits who had no clear view of their future career lines. Parental direction had either been absent or had swung to the other extreme of perfectionism; in the latter instance it seemed that the parents were concerned primarily with the projection of a son or daughter as their representative, through whom they might live vicariously and who would compensate for their own thwarted ambitions. In the majority of cases it was not difficult to establish a clear-cut neurotic basis for academic failure. Accordingly, the sensible frame of reference in which to place these failures seemed to be a psychiatric one. The usual debate ensued over where the line should be drawn with respect to conscious personal responsibility on the one hand and unconscious neurotic process on the other. The feeling remained, however, that many students, who otherwise would continue in ignorance of the sources of their failures, could be helped to re-orient themselves by the University's placing the entire process of academic leave in a psychiatric framework. It was felt this would delineate for the student the true nature of his difficulties. The practice was consequently instituted of referring each such student for psychiatric evaluation, placing him on leave of absence "for medical reasons," and if possible referring him for psychotherapy during the period of leave. Should he wish to return to active standing at the end of this period he was to be screened by the psychiatrist who might then recommend termination of the medical leave.

The rationale for this latter procedure, of course, was the assumption that the psychiatrist was best equipped to assess the resolution of the student's neurotic pattern. Experience, however, soon demonstrated that this arrangement was unworkable. First, a single interview, even under ideal circumstances of neutrality, may be highly deceptive. Second, the circumstances were all but neutral, in that the psychiatrist was in effect, and despite himself, the person who would pass on the student's reinstatement: the Administration was very unlikely to act contrary to his recommendation. As a further logical extension of this policy, students for whom disciplinary action was pending were also referred to the psychiatrist, often, it seemed, in a semi-enforced manner, but again with the benevolent motive of helping the student at a point of crisis to clarify for himself the inner difficulties which had led him to this point. Again, and somewhat inadvertently, the psychiatrist assumed the role of gatekeeper, even though officially the Dean's office of course continued to make all administrative decisions and to be responsible for all administrative action.

Finally, the role of the psychiatrist in relation to new admissions had similar questionable aspects. Each new student was customarily accepted for admission pending clearance by the Medical Department. This involved submitting a Health Record and, when indicated, coming for a personal examination. While there could be no reasonable objection to the screening out of students who presented themselves for admission in a frankly psychotic state, a dilemma of conscience often arose when a student had been accepted by the Admissions Committee and then revealed on his Health Record a history of major psychiatric illness. Such students were interviewed by the psychiatrist who, though often in serious doubt about their prospects for academic success, never in fact exercised his prerogative of rejection for medical reasons. The dilemma he had to face in each of these cases was whether to spare a student almost certain failure or whether to allow him access to learning from this failure; the second alternative seemed more promising. Beyond this, needless to say, the best psychiatric judgment can err in predicting the future; one is every so often pleasantly amazed at a patient's doing the "impossible."

The course actually adopted was to urge these students to avail themselves of the clinical facilities on the campus early in the school year, with the accent placed on prophylaxis. Often a few early consultations seemed to sustain a student through the crisis of transition from home to college or from college to graduate school; for some this suggestion led to their beginning regular therapy early in their school careers, when it was likely to be most effective. Others, of course, proved unable to cope with the college situation, but for these, and perhaps especially for these, early consultation was of value by helping them to accept in a thoroughgoing fashion their current shortcomings and to work out a constructive therapeutic or alternative vocational program.

The student body was not — and could not be — aware of the fact that the psychiatrist rarely barred anyone from admission or re-admission and never recommended that a student be permanently severed. However, they soon realized, accurately, that in a variety of crucial situations the effective power of decision was actually placed in his hands and that this ran counter to the Administration's officially stated policy. They were not slow in discerning the objectionable aspects of this procedure and in expressing their objections openly. Students coming to the Counseling Center or to the psychiatrist expressed much stronger doubts than their usual ones about the confidentiality in which their communications were held; many distorted reports and even entirely unfounded rumors began to circulate in this atmosphere of growing distrust and confusion; there was simultaneously a definite drop in the number of new referrals. The issue was picked up and pursued by some of the student leaders and finally the college newspaper openly attacked the clinical services as "axemen for the Administration."

The adolescent's inclination to fight any real or imagined

restriction of his freedom imposed by those *in loco parentis* had doubtless contributed to the vehemence of the student's reaction and helped to make of the issue a "cause." Nevertheless, their complaints did touch on a valid issue, and they did not merely protest but made responsible efforts directed at the clarification of the total situation. This helped to heighten our awareness of the fact that an unequivocal and public policy was a necessary condition for sustaining a level of student trust sufficient for effective clinical functioning. The Administration, the Psychiatrist, and the Counseling Center responded by systematically re-examining in common meetings their policies and practices in the light of desired goals and probable effects; the students were informed that, once formulated, these policies would be made public in all details. They were assured that, with the exception of true emergencies, the nature of which was spelled out, confidentiality was sacred and the role of the psychiatrist and of the counsellor in relation to individual students would be purely clinical. The furor promptly subsided and individual therapeutic work seemed to proceed with a new degree of freedom. This experience illustrates the principle that when students register legitimate and responsible complaints about their school it behooves an administration to consider seriously its own shortcomings in as democratic a fashion as possible.

In reformulating our policies and practices we aimed at retaining the advantages offered by a psychiatric consultation at critical points in a student's career, but within a framework that would clearly separate the clinical from the administrative functions.

First, with regard to students facing possible disciplinary action, the following policy was established: "These students should not be referred to the psychiatrist or to the Counseling Center until an administrative decision has been reached and the student informed of it. Following this, if the student seems at all motivated, the availability of clinical facilities should be underlined for him, with care taken that he understand clearly that the referral is elective on his part." This should counteract any misunderstandings about the role of the psychiatrist on the campus while preserving the useful features of referring students to clinical facilities at points of crisis.

Some of these students, although giving clear indications of being in need of therapeutic help, are not amenable at the time to elective referral to the psychiatrist or the Counseling Center. For many of such students a fairly prolonged contact with a member of the Office of Student Personnel has proved very beneficial. In addition to immediate help with the presenting difficulty, such contact provides the students with a "free" situation in which they may ultimately come to recognize the need for professional assistance. Usually, with patience, such refractory, basically frightened, students can be brought smoothly and effectively to an ultimate clinical referral. Much more referral loss seems to occur when an anxious administrator attempts to refer a student precipitously. In keeping with our general impression of student attitudes, we expect that most students at these points of crisis will welcome the suggestion of referral. However, even when it is not possible to help students arrive at this decision the alternative of a forced, or semi-forced administrative referral is not the solution of the difficulty. It appears from experience that most students referred under real or imagined duress are not able to relate freely enough to the clinician to benefit from the referral to any significant extent. This is most unequivocal with students for whom some administrative action is pending. The psychiatrist is seen here as having the decision in his hands unilaterally. Needless to say, the student under these circumstances withholds information which he feels would affect the administrative decision adversely. It is often just this information which is crucial to an accurate clinical assessment.

The initially established procedures concerning leaves of absence were also revised and a policy drafted which reads, in part, as follows: "Except for instances of clear-cut mental breakdown, with unmistakable severe overt symptomatology, it is suggested that the majority of students previously granted 'medical leave of absence for psychiatric reasons' now be granted 'leave for personal reasons' *at the discretion of the administration.* In order to avoid confusion for the student as to who makes admission and readmission decisions, and, more importantly in order to put the criteria for readmission in the proper frame of reference, all such decisions should be made exclusively by the Dean's Office, prior to any clinical referral. In this way the legitimate criteria for readmission, namely real accomplishment during the period of leave, would be assessed by those best able to do so. Referral to the college psychiatrist, after leave has been granted, would thus be fully elective." In the setting defined by this policy, if the student accepts the referral, attention can be focused efficiently on defining with him the underlying unconscious motivations for his difficulties; if as a result he should seek therapy it would be on his own initiative. Therapy during the leave would thus be divorced from the readmission decision, as it must be for any effectiveness.

In order not to be shackled into inflexibility by formal policy, arrangements can be made, in exceptional cases, for the psychiatrist to communicate certain of his impressions to the Administration, provided he and the student agree that this is desirable and also agree on the content of the communication.

In summary, we feel that a university psychiatric service must state its policies clearly, unambiguously, and publicly. These policies must embody the cardinal principles of confidentiality and of separation of clinical from administrative functions. Except in the most clear-cut emergencies, we feel the psychiatrist should abstain from any action which might have direct bearing on a student's administrative standing. Essential to the success of such a program is the education of the administrative personnel in the proper techniques of making referrals which would be truly elective for the student.

III

SPECIFIC FEATURES OF THERAPEUTIC WORK ON A SMALL CAMPUS

Eugenia Hanfmann, Elliot Baker, Richard M. Jones

One of the ways to make brief psychotherapy more effective is to take into account the setting in which treatment takes place, avoiding the pitfalls it presents and utilizing its favorable features. College counseling deals with people who are not only passing through the same developmental stage but are also sharing a well defined life-situation. This report deals with the impact on counseling of situations typical of a relatively small coeducational liberal arts college offering free psychological counseling service on campus. Before listing the aspects of the college situation that shape counseling practices, we shall briefly summarize the main features of the Brandeis Counseling Center at which these observations were made.

The Counseling Center, now in its eleventh year of existence and well established on campus, is attached to the Department of Psychology. It is staffed by several well-trained clinical psychologists, some of whom are also teachers, and has its own psychiatric consultant, as well as a Visiting Committee made up of prominent local psychiatrists. The Center is open to all students, but the severely disturbed as well as those needing medical study can be referred to the psychiatrist on the staff of the Health Office. This distribution of functions leaves the Center staff free to work with the students who can be helped within limited time: those going through healthy adolescent crises and those showing neurotic personality patterns. Whenever possible the estimated long term cases among the latter are referred to private therapists; this often requires a period of preparatory work. Students likely to benefit from counseling are entitled under the terms of their enrollment to one weekly hour for a period of up to one academic year; more time is provided when it seems necessary and is feasible. At the end of the period of counseling those students who decide to continue therapy are helped to make contacts with clinics and with private therapists.

The Center is run purely as a counseling service for students. It is not used for training graduate students and it does not give or evaluate psychological tests. There are no formalized intake procedures, and there are no waiting lists, except for brief periods when the demand is at a peak. Full confidentiality of counseling discussions is assured. The names of students coming to the Center are not reported to the Administration. In the rare cases when need for some communication arises this is discussed with the student. The service is made known to the entering students in various ways, including brief informational talks by the staff members and a detailed description in the Student Handbook. Effective ways of referring students to the Center are discussed with the Resident Counselors in the dormitories and the staff of the Student Personnel Office; they are also provided with booklets of questions and answers about the service compiled from typical questions asked by the students.

The method and the extent of the work done at the Center vary with the case. Our procedures range from an hour of simple listening or of active realistic discussion through prolonged but merely supportive contacts to intensive work bringing to light preconscious, and occasionally unconscious, material. The majority of the counselors have been analytically trained, with Freudian or neo-Freudian orientation, and their work with typical cases can be described as analytically oriented brief therapy. We often find that the students go much farther in a short time than is usually considered possible. We follow each

Specific Features of Therapeutic Work

as far, or as "deep," as he wants to go, except when this course is contra-indicated because of intense transference or of some negative reactions to movement that are difficult to work out within the given time limit.

In the following discussions we shall dwell neither on the features of adolescence as such, nor on the criteria we use in trying to fit the therapeutic approach to the dynamics of an individual case. Starting with the decision whether to accept a student for counseling, evaluations and choices of this kind are of course made constantly by the counselor, implicitly and explicitly, by himself, and in discussions with colleagues, but this is not peculiar to college counseling as such. We shall discuss only those determinants of our practices that are rooted in the typical features of the college situation which affect a large proportion of students. The specific features pertinent to our work are the following.

Attendance at a residential school both emphasizes and furthers *the loosening of a student's dependence on his family*. Although his financial dependence usually continues and the tie to the family is expressed and maintained through periodical returns home, his day-to-day living at school is outside of parental knowledge and control. This transitional situation is strikingly expressed in the behavior of some students who develop dual ways of feeling and acting in the two situations: more mature in school and more childish at home.

Although college life offers large areas of personal freedom, some of the functions of the waning *parental control* are *transferred to the school* itself; this transfer is both an institutional fact, expressed in formalized guidance, evaluations, rules, discipline, and a part of the students' own feelings. Colleges differ in the amount and nature of control they exercise, but in most of them the analogues of some of the parental functions — e.g. of model and discipliner — tend to be institutionally distributed between faculty and administration; the "parental figures" are numerous and varied, giving the student a wide range of choice.

Important as the parents and the college authorities are for the student, most of their free time is filled by *interaction with age-equals*. Shared living and interests permit a wide range of personal relations, from superficial to close, including heterosexual friendships. Participation in groups, large and small, organized and informal, provides opportunity for extensive sharing of experience, for leadership, prestige, and for the shaping of "public opinion." There are no fraternities in this particular school, but the "intellectuals," the "radicals," the "bohemians," the "athletes," the "socialites," are easily identified by the students.

Among the various media of personal interaction the mode of *intellectual discussion* occupies an outstanding place in school, both among students and between students and faculty; in our particular school there is also an emphasis on creativity and artistic expression. Of specific importance in our context is the great popularity of psychology in the student culture. The students flock to the courses that attempt to give them some insight into their personal dynamics; theories of mental health are widely discussed in the classroom and outside. Although in the faculty as a whole the knowledge of and the attitude toward psychological treatment vary widely, a positive image of the pursuit of self-knowledge is likely to emerge in the school environment.

The fact that membership in the college community can be terminated by academic failure or expulsion for bad conduct, as well as voluntarily, is often pertinent for the design of counseling. For the majority of students the total time to be spent in college is clearly defined in advance; within these time limits, periods at school alternate with periods away from it, which usually means away from the area.

The college *counselor* unlike his colleagues in clinics and in private practice, is an integral *part of the closed community* he serves, and his institutional role may be variously interpreted by the students. He may be personally known to some of them through contact in classes or at some college functions, and he is likely to know some of the friends and teachers of the students he counsels. The counselor also has access to the official record of the student, and he can try, if he chooses, to influence administrative decisions about students. These circumstances, while increasing the information available to the counselor, may lead to a variety of feelings and of conflicts, both in the students and in the counselors.

To summarize, the psychological counselor in a relatively small campus school draws his clients from a closed society, the members of which have a variety of relations among themselves. This society, devoted to the pursuit of knowledge, is institutionally organized along quasi-familial lines and replaces, in part, the family, the tie to which is weakening. The counselor himself, though autonomous in his capacity of therapist, is a member of this community; and his contact with the client is predicated on the latter's continuance as a student, is subject to an arbitrary time limit, and is punctuated by interruptions at vacation times.

In the following sections we shall attempt to show the bearing of these factors on the various stages of the counseling process: the initiation of the contact, the period of induction into therapy, the period of counseling proper, and finally its termination, sometimes followed by referral. The discussion will center on the problems these situational features may create for counseling, and on their possible therapeutic utilization.

1. Initiation of Counseling

As a result of the information given to the entering students, the majority of them realize that opportunity for obtaining psychological help exists on campus; they know that the service is free of charge, confidential, different from other kinds of college counseling, and that it can be approached directly by the students themselves. If this advance information is meaningless for some, psychology courses or conversations with friends may later fill it with meaning. Many come to the Center via courses or via volunteer work done by the students in local mental hospitals. Discussions of psychological theories and methods not only strengthen motivation for self-exploration but also provide some anxious students with face-saving devices for approaching the Center. Many a contact of ostensibly academic nature turns into a counseling session.

The location of the Center on campus and the informality of procedure make it quickly accessible to the students. Although they are ordinarily asked to call or write for an appointment, those who simply come in on the spur of the moment often can be seen right away, if only briefly. Thus, it happens that some students come in when they are under the impact of a recent traumatic event. A break-up or quarrel with a boy or girl friend, or an examination panic, may lower the resistance to therapy, which would be reinstated if more time were permitted to pass after the upset. Occasionally friends of the student take matters in hand in such a crisis and bring him or her to the Center.

Participation of friends in the student's decision to enter counseling is an outstanding feature of a campus school. The majority of those students who have worked successfully in counseling tell about it to a few intimate friends; they are often active in referring others and in counteracting the stigma attached to getting help. This first-hand information and personal advice from peers is much more effective than any formal informational talks. If one stops to consider that at any given time about one third of the students in school have been or are in touch with the Center the importance of this source of re-

Specific Features of Therapeutic Work 49

ferrals becomes obvious. Many more students come to the Center on advice of friends, or with the support of friends, than through any other channels on campus.

There is, however, a reverse side to each of the factors that ordinarily facilitate the initiation of counseling. If the Center's location makes it easily accessible, it also precludes absolute privacy: the student may be seen entering it, or meet acquaintances within. Although such encounters often result in release and relief ("Oh, you too — the best adjusted girl on campus!") they may be dreaded in anticipation. It cannot be known how many students are kept away by the fear of discovery, but we know that some are greatly delayed in coming.

If praise of the Center tends to spread in the college community, any unfavorable opinion or rumor travels even faster and farther. A student who after a tentative approach has decided against counseling may tell his friends that he found the counselors not sufficiently psychoanalytic or dynamic; a temporary upset may make him feel that counseling makes him worse; distorted versions of what a counselor said in a session occasionally come back to him through others, and of course in many cases do not.

This easy spread of information and misinformation is not too deleterious to our work as long as unfavorable opinion is amply outweighed by its opposite, but it creates special problems in respect to those students who are given to distortion and to acting out. They are easily tempted to strike back at the Center whenever they feel let down by the counselor for a real or fantasied reason. In one extreme case the Center was deluged by telephone calls from friends, physicians, and faculty members, each of whom had received from the student a different but equally alarming version of what took place in the sessions. The counselor may be able to meet this challenge and turn it to therapeutic advantage, but in deciding on whether "intra-mural" or "extra-mural" treatment is indicated, the student's potential for creating a disturbance on campus should be taken into account.

An obstacle to counseling not to be considered lightly arises from the center's being an integral part of an institution where traditionally each student's career is a matter of official record. When a service is first introduced that claims to enjoy the right of privileged communication, this claim is met with understandable distrust by the students. This problem looms large in a small campus school where the fact of personal interaction among the staff is obvious to the students; it may be intensified if the same service that counsels the normal majority must also deal with the severely disturbed whose situation often requires administrative decisions.

During the first years of the Center's work we met with many misgivings, and with many requests for special safeguards of privacy. Even apparently trustful students were easily made suspicious by any slight suggestion of the Center's connection with other school offices: it was almost taboo for the counselors to stop for a chat with a member of the administration on campus. In some cases the counseling process did not really get under way until some unplanned-for incident signified to the student that the matter of confidentiality was taken seriously by the counselor. It is indicative of the students' expectations that some of them, on eventually perceiving the Center's autonomy from the Administration, hypothesized that the service was sponsored and financed by some outside agency and not by the school.

Fortunately this obstacle to counseling can be thoroughly if not speedily overcome if the service is able to live up to its promises without a break. Once its reputation for reliability is established, chance rumors to the contrary will have only a temporary effect on the majority of the students. The issue remains a special problem of the overly suspicious and of those few who feel with some reason that they have a dangerous secret to hide. Many of those who seek therapy outside the school, without mediation of the Center or the Health Office, are presumably recruited from this group. Those who come to the Center usually test out the counselor, indirectly or openly. If the counselor passes the test, without committing himself to the untenable position that he would never, under any circumstances, break confidentiality, the issue is usually resolved.

The institutional position of the service presents an obstacle of a different kind to those students who are concerned less with the issue of safety than with that of values. Among them are many whose rebellion against parental and other authority takes the form of an ideological struggle against any opinions or standards which they feel are enforced from above. Depending on their personal casting of agents and victims of tyranny, or tradition-bound and free men, the psychologists *qua* therapists may find themselves in one of the categories. If they are viewed as servants of the powers that be they may be despised or feared as "secret persuaders." This apprehension, which in some degree is present in very many students, leads some of them to explore the counselor's political and philosophical views, but it is seldom an obstacle to counseling once personal rapport has been established. It is however a matter of record that the most prominent "revolutionaries" of the school, the leaders in any fight against the administration, do not appear at the Center, except in case of breakdown. To a lesser extent, this is also true of those who identify themselves with the beatniks.

While the influence of friends often facilitates the initiation of counseling, some aspects of this "shared enterprise" create problems, which must be discerned and handled from the start. Two or more students may apply for counseling who are not "just friends" but more intimately related: a boy and a girl friend, two rivals, roommates who are close or mutually hostile, members of a close-knit clique. Their stated purposes in coming may be interrelated, as in the case of a couple having trouble, or they may be individual and separate. But regardless of the stated purpose, the fact of the other's coming for counseling also is meaningful to each in many ways, conscious and unconscious. To avoid possible complications we ask each newcomer whether any of his close friends is attending the Center, and if so, assign him to a different counselor. This represents a qualification of our usual policy of accepting when feasible a student's expressed preference for working with a particular counselor.

There are other facts of school life to be considered in conjunction with the problem presented by the student in his first contact. Is he in good standing academically, or is there a chance that he may be dropped by the school within the next term? If so, or if he graduates at the end of the year, what are his plans for the near future? Is he likely to stay in the area, and for how long? How much time is there to the end of the school year? Answers to these questions help to determine whether school counseling can be profitable at the given time, and the pros and contras can be discussed with the student. If he comes to the Center close to the end of the academic year with a difficulty of old standing and of wide import, this may represent an ineffective compromise between seeking and rejecting help, which can be brought to his awareness. In such cases it is often more advisable after clarification to postpone the beginning of counseling to the fall and ensure the possibility of continuance than to accept the limits the student set by the time he chose for coming. This of course does not apply to emergencies, to situations where the student (often a senior) faces an immediate important decision, or to problems that seem capable of solution through a short period of work.

2. The Pre-counseling Period

The college environment, instead of being conducive to rationalized *avoidance of* therapy, in which an initial contact may be taken to signify a certain state of motivated readiness, can be conducive to rationalized *approach to* therapy. Here the initial contact signifies a deployed state of readiness and unreadiness in some initially unknown ratio. The situation of the college counselor is in this one respect sometimes not unlike that of his colleagues at the other end of the social spectrum in prisons, court agencies, etc.: the fact that a new client is sitting before him does not on its face reflect anything specific with regard to what the client is or may in future be ready and willing to do there. Intensive work is very often accomplished from the first session, and what may seem to the counselor to be naïveté in the student's approach to counseling often turns out to have been merely its tacit acceptance as a plausible means to the solution of personal problems. In the present section we shall focus on instances in which the initial contact is mitigated by varieties of resistance not routinely encountered in other clinical settings, which require a corresponding variety of preparatory counseling methods.

It sometimes happens, for example, that a student comes to the Counseling Center avowedly shopping. He knows he has it coming to him, he states, and doesn't want to pass it up if it is something he can profit from. Of many of these it is genuinely true that nothing is back of the manner of contact but lack of first-hand experience with professional counseling. Thorough exploration of typical problem areas and sensitive demonstration in the first hour of what may be expected in counseling is usually the best way of responding to this approach. It has the merit of being a clarifying experience if that is all that is required, and a stimulant to active resistances if these are latent. With due respect for "client-centered" schools of thought we find a non-directive approach in the first session to be merely confusing to a student who simply doesn't know what psychological counseling is.

It not infrequently happens, however, that between the shopping approach and acceptance of counseling as a responsible way to the solution of personal problems there exists a covert line of resistance: the student sees himself in the role of enterprising scholar, or broadminded critic. He has learned of the various schools of psychotherapy, and wants to see if he can identify the counselor's techniques, or he "doesn't believe in Freud," but wants to give psychoanalysis the benefit of the doubt, etc. In an educational setting it is usually advisable, once the counselor has recognized the defensive implications in back of the manner of approach, not to bring the student's attention to them immediately. Rather in these instances it seems best to enter freely and lightly for a time into intellectual discussions of the various therapies, of individualism, conformity, Zen, of the fate of creativity in psychoanalysis, etc.: sandwiching between these discussions sufficient tentative demonstration of how *his particular* therapy would proceed, so that in a few sessions either the student confronts himself with the covert strings he has placed on the counseling sessions, or the counselor may do so. A renewed agreement can then be worked out, if the student wishes to continue, in which academic matters are to be left to the classroom and the counseling sessions are to concentrate on personal issues.

Other motives for coming to the Center which may emerge by implication in the first sessions include: wishing to get an excuse to use in the handling of teachers or administrators; to get a boy- or girl-friend into therapy, in order to change him or her; to prove to friends that counseling is nonsense; to share in a fad; to meet the counselor who is seeing or has seen a friend

Specific Features of Therapeutic Work

or roommate — sometimes to tell his or her side of the story. The place in the student's emotional economy of these pre-arranged restraints on counseling varies. They may be a weakly held device for getting past the door, or may reflect a brittle system of defenses. The length of the preliminary period, the methods employed during this period, and the specific features of the college environment which bear on it, therefore, also vary.

Commonly underlying the various guises that may serve to initiate contact is the familiar ego-protective attitude that therapy is an externally administered procedure, an artifice or technique to which one submits with expectations (both hoped for and feared) of being changed. Therefore the goal of the pre-counseling period is a redefined agreement between counselor and student, which includes an informed and responsible commitment on the student's part to the prospect of mutually guided intra-personal changes in certain specified directions. Usually a more or less officious clarification of policy is the best means of beginning this work: emphasis on the necessity of free choice in the decision to enter counseling, clarification of university policy as regards the freedom of the counseling staff from administrative direction, emphasis on professional confidentiality with reference to teachers, parents, or the student himself who may by implication be seeking to be made an exception in the case of someone else, etc.

As the student begins to appreciate the realistic workings and limitations of counseling, and as the counselor's strategically interspersed demonstrations begin to appeal to some inner sense of direction, a variety of more personally toned reservations may be expected to emerge which anticipate a positive turning point: "I've enjoyed talking with you the last few weeks, but I feel guilty taking up your time. I'm sure that there are plenty of others who need it more than I." Or, "I guess I mustn't be too disturbed or you'd have sent me to a psychiatrist by now, right? By the way, what actually *is* the difference between a psychologist and a psychiatrist?" Some stated or implied variant of "do *I* really need counseling" is the most frequent sign that the turning point is near. In the majority of cases the question is to be taken to mean not "do I really *need* it," but "am I really *worth* it," and should be handled accordingly. One student, for example, at the conclusion of a year's very constructive work, said, "You know, when I really began to trust you and go into things was when I asked if I really needed this, and all you said was 'yes'. I think that was the first time any grown-up ever expressed *confidence* in me."

In the majority of cases requiring a period of pre-counseling the turning point comes in the first three or four meetings. The student may begin a session by openly disavowing his reservations; as often as not the disavowal is implied in his simply going to work in earnest. In either instance the counselor does well to acknowledge the transition, openly by re-clarifying the agreement, or tacitly on his part by intensifying his own contribution to the session. One of us who had inherited an oddly partitioned office found it both appropriate and effective to acknowledge the turning point by suggesting that further sessions be held in the more comfortably appointed half of the office — a feature we do not recommend as the couch of counseling, but only record as an instructive observation.

Preliminary working through of a student's surface reservations does not in all cases result in a smooth transition into counseling proper. For example after a few sessions the student may fortify himself with finality behind the attitude usually expressed in passing in the first session that receiving professional help is a sign of weakness. When academic standing is tenuous, or a quick referral seems advisable, we have felt called upon to refute this position, pointing out that not receiving help when it is clearly needed, so far from signifying strength, shows stupidity. As a rule, however, it is best to count this as either a first turning point or as a therapeutic failure, and to see it on either count as an opportunity to reassure the student of his autonomy in the relationship. Admittedly the line between such reassurance and rejection of the student as unworthy of counseling is sometimes a thin one, revealing itself only to intuition.

Other such temporary or final terminations include letting the counselor down easy ("very helpful but perhaps when I have more time"); disavowal without commitment ("I guess I just did want to see what it was like. Now if I ever need it I'll know"); or conflict with parents ("they say I'm crazy, that I need nothing of the kind, so I'd better stop"). In a college setting, as the meaning of an initial contact is not precise neither is the meaning of an interruption or an alleged termination. The very redefinition of the agreement toward which the counselor had been working in the preliminary sessions must sometimes be ritualized, as it were, by going out in order to come in again. Sometimes a period of going it alone after a few exploratory sessions is seen in retrospect to have been an essential part of the pre-counseling phase, which ushered in a really constructive period of intensive work. It also pays not to overlook the effect on college counseling of the specific developmental crisis characteristic of the client population, the emergence of independent identity. While this feeling frequently vies at deeper levels with stronger needs to be dependent and selfless, which may often be threatened in the counseling relationship, it is not by any means always the case that a desire to be independent of counseling is most aptly viewed as resistance. Also, while it is not true that skilled psychotherapy is a technical artifice to which one can become addicted, it is equally not true that it affords the most natural of all possible ways by which people grow. It is therefore well to respect the grains of reality often inherent in these resistances.

A student's decision to withdraw after a few exploratory

sessions is sometimes *not* discussed with the counselor, but is summarily communicated by phone or by message. Again this may signify a counseling failure or a need on the part of the student to prepare himself at his own pace and in his own way for a more earnest involvement in further work. In these instances we have learned to keep the door ajar by note.

In rare cases the period of pre-counseling neither leads in a few sessions into counseling proper nor to an abrupt termination or interruption but extends over a lengthy period during which the only feasible goal is the resolution of ambivalence toward professional help. We count the challenges in such cases among the most exacting as regards the personal and technical virtuosity required of the counselor. Correspondingly, success in such cases is most rewarding. It bears noting that therapeutic challenges of this nature are unique to a *free* and easily accessible counseling service. When such a student is ready for referral we find it advisable to call on the services of private therapists whose previous experience permits them to appreciate the peculiar problems to be considered in the transfer.

Bearing significantly on the pre-counseling period are several environmental features specific to college counseling. Inevitable campus meetings between counselor and the students who are trying it on their own may be used to advantage and to disadvantage. These constitute particularly sensitive day-to-day challenges best left to the counselor's intuition. There are times, for example, when a student's attempt to avert a meeting of eyes should be taken at face value, and there are times when it constitutes an invitation to be recognized, which may be followed by an inquiry about the counselor's schedule. There are no rules of thumb in these situations.

On a small campus the public and private information at the counselor's disposal with respect to students he has seen, is seeing, or will see may be used to advantage. A boy previously seen in a few exploratory sessions comes afoul of the law, making a brief written invitation to resume counseling appropriate. Or a girl who had figured prominently in the sessions of two separate severely disturbed individuals finally comes in person, and the counselor is prepared in the first session to explore her affinity for pathology.

The ease with which students may enter counseling without their parents' knowledge has the occasional disadvantage of making it possible for a student to seduce himself into an emotional situation for which he is not prepared. These are usually situations in which the student cannot from the first session refrain from expressing unabashed hatred toward his parents, and also cannot defend himself against the guilt that is consequent on doing so. In these cases the preliminary work consists of preparing the student to confront his parents with the step he has taken, after which the counseling may be containably continued. The strategically placed Thanksgiving, Christmas and spring vacations usually spent at home are useful in facilitating such family crises. Many students, although needing the freedom to take the initial step without parental approval, nevertheless can only take up their problems in *earnest* after they have been able to clear it at home. Conversely an occasional student who has been pressed into counseling by his parents may feel compelled to discontinue — and to return without their knowledge at a later date — in order to settle independently into responsible work.

The absence of intake procedures and the relative informality possible with a small staff has allowed for quite versatile handling of the preliminary period in certain atypical cases. For example, after several unprofitable attempts to begin counseling at the pressured suggestion of friends and teachers, one very ambivalent girl finally arranged an appointment independently with a counselor who she knew could see her only once because of conflicting commitments. In that session she was able, plaintively, to write out why the prospect of discussing her problem was so painful: "I masturbate!" Assured that she could continue counseling with a staff member who would already have seen her note she was able to begin work without the excessive burden of having either to conceal or reveal her secret, and the permanent counselor was in a position to raise the troublesome issue after progress had been made on other issues.

The fact that some of the staff members also teach courses sometimes results in the preliminary work being conducted within the framework of teacher-student conferences. Most students, having made the contact by this route, can be brought at the turning point to see the logic of not mixing personal with academic matters, and transfer to another staff member can be arranged with relative ease. Occasionally, however, either the course work or the counseling is sacrificed in the process. One boy who was nearing the end of his college career and was about to enter marriage with overwhelming trepidation steadfastly refused to make the suggested transfer to another counselor, and finally decided to drop a course he was taking with the counselor in order to go to work on his personal problems. Conversely, a gifted girl, after impulsively revealing to her teacher an account of her troubled sex life, took his suggestion to enter counseling with another staff member, as she would have to forego two important courses if she made the present teacher a counselor. It developed later that she had not been ready at that time to make optimal use of counseling, the outburst having been motivated more by a crush on the teacher than a desire for help.

Finally, it should be emphasized that during the course of preliminary work the counselor has an opportunity to determine the role that therapy is likely to play in the student's future as well as in his present. The issues involved are partly diagnostic, partly prognostic, and partly of a reality assessment nature: does the student seem nearly ready for optimally intensive work? Will he probably decide to continue at a later date? Will the opportunity and necessary resources be available? The number of permutations made possible by varying degrees of present readiness, present and future needs, and present and future opportunities prohibits their adequate coverage here. Suffice it to say that in a college setting contact with the counseling center is usually a person's first independent experience with psychotherapy; its introduction should therefore be tailored not only to immediate considerations but also to future redefinitions of professional help at probable short and long ranges.

3. The Course of Counseling

Once counseling proper gets under way the situational factors which loomed large in the shaping of the initial stage may recede into the background. The process is carried by its own momentum, and the events of school life serve mainly as material for observation by the student of his own personal and interpersonal functioning. Because of this personal focusing and the resulting idiosyncratic selection of what is reported, no coherent picture of college life as a whole emerges for the therapist from the cumulative reports of the students.[1] Yet for all students some sets of factors within the reality situation are invested with great personal significance because of their pertinence to the typical problems of adolescence. Since the Center is closely integrated with the school, and consequently with the life situation of the student, these factors are not merely reflected in the content of the sessions: they may enter the counseling situation more directly, in their own right, and either further or hinder the process. In the following sections we shall discuss the three

[1] There is no realistic basis for the fantasies occasionally entertained by faculty or administration, that the Center functions as an informal student opinion poll and is a repository of rich information pertinent to the running of the school. Except in cases of spectacular events the counselors get only occasional hints of school matters that would be of general or practical interest.

main groups that often have to be reckoned with not only at the start and at the end but intermittently during the total course of counseling: students' parents, college authorities, and fellow students.

A. Parents

Relationships with the family form a large segment of the students' current life. The conflicts which are often to the fore are contemporary and are fought through with real people whose involvement in the struggle sometimes equals that of the student. Being a part of the adolescent's growth process these conflicts are open, alive and in flux; they are easily brought into counseling and may strongly influence its course and progress. While historic probing lends perspective to the student's self-understanding, it is the analysis of current experiences that provides checks for misconceptions and fantasies and often leads to most productive results. Visits at home, which punctuate the year for most students, present therapeutic opportunities not to be overlooked.

The first return home after having entered college may be particularly illuminating for the student: he views his family for the first time from the vantage point of a more independent status, within a changed frame of reference. In cases of acutely homesick freshmen the first, often precipitate, return home may bring about the decision to withdraw from school, or else to try and "stick it out" away from home. The timing of this first visit and the preparation for it achieved in counseling may be important in determining his choice. When shame over personal defeat, or fear of hurting parents by failure, loom large as obstacles to fleeing from school, the student is immobilized between two negative alternatives. After facing this conflict in counseling he may be able, on his first visit home, to be more open to the evidence of his family's feelings. If he discovers that his withdrawal from the out-of-town school is not viewed

Specific Features of Therapeutic Work

as disastrous, he may be set free to choose his course in terms of his own readiness to leave home. If his homesickness does not amount to panic the student may be able to postpone the visit home long enough to give the school a chance, to become more clearly aware of his feelings, and to prepare himself to take a closer look at the home situation.

In one such case of acute homesickness, exploration showed that the student felt left out, hurt and resentful towards her parents for continuing their life without her. She wanted to remain a little girl who shared all her secrets and joys with her family and was the center of their world. She struggled ambivalently about going home to visit, wanting the counselor to give her permission to do so. When she finally did go she discovered that both home and her mother were less perfect than she had thought. She painfully realized that she was growing up, and that her interests and values were becoming different from her family's. She returned from the visit prepared to accept these changes.

Sometimes a visit home after a longer separation seems to be necessary to precipitate the emergence of insights prepared by counseling, or to make these insights bear fruit. Thus a girl who felt guilty that she could not be the kind of person she thought her mother wanted discovered the reasons for these feelings during the year of counseling; no significant change took place, however, until she went home during spring vacation. There she developed the simple but powerful realization that she was actually very different from her mother. Prolonged separation from home and re-entry with more self-understanding made the obvious apparent to her.

While physical separation may promote individuation, the recurrent contacts with parents give the student a chance to experience himself in interaction with them and to observe its effects on himself. Sometimes an unbroken continuity between the past and the present permits a direct observation of significant patterns which makes clear to the adolescent some of the causal connections operating in his development.

A girl who was struggling for her autonomy persistently denied the importance of certain childhood experiences: to give them weight meant blaming her mother and excusing herself from responsibility for her problems. Yet her contemporary, and thus meaningful, struggles with her mother did gradually clarify for her the nature of their interactions. The mother, a critical and demanding person, wrote bitter denouncing letters complaining of her daughter's forsaking her, demanded confidences from her, and sought to enlist the counselors on her side of the struggle. The impact of these experiences enabled the daughter to see that the mother's hold on her was based on a fostering of her guilt feelings, and she took courage to oppose this entanglement.

At a certain point in counseling the student may take active steps to test his or her fantasies about the parents.

A student imagined that her brilliant father would never believe that she had problems. After her own disappointment in herself had been explored, she timidly told him that she had been seeing a counselor. She was amazed to learn that he was aware of her problems but had felt hesitant to discuss them; he accepted her wish to be independent of his influence and was pleased with the initiative she had taken in seeking help.

The students' attempts at clarifying parental images are often accompanied by attempts to share and check their discoveries with the parents, or to face them openly with their grievances.

Specific Features of Therapeutic Work

Such attempts may fail at first, or lead to increased strife. Often, however, the parents will respond to the student's new frankness in kind. A chain reaction of mutual growth may result.

Hand in hand with attempts at mutual understanding go attempts at changing one's pattern of behavior towards the parents, for which successive visits at home provide opportunities.

> A girl, who demanded intellectual achievement and perfection from herself, denied her frustrated dependency needs and insisted that her family could not function without her being subservient to their needs. She allowed herself to become judge and arbiter of all family conflicts, and felt that her goodness would some day bring its rewards. In counseling she became increasingly aware of her selflessness and her fear of standing alone. She had convinced herself that her actions were valuable for the family. During a vacation, when she made a more careful examination of her experiences at home, this myth was exploded. On the next trip home she attempted to give up her customary role and to act as a person in her own right, desisting from her former strenuous attempts to please and help everyone.

Occasionally, the relationship to a parent is perceived in a new light and modified only after a clarification of the central pattern has taken place in the transference, accompanied by a release of emotions. The actual contact with the parent serves to complete or further the change. The two examples that follow exemplify this course.

> A boy who perceived his father as a powerful, angry man came into counseling in danger of failing; he felt inadequate and unable to meet his father's expectations. Anticipating criticism from the counselor, he openly labelled him as being

like his father and soon found himself unable to participate in the sessions actively: he had hoped that it was the counselor who would "analyze" and change him. When his dependent demands were not met, he felt anxiety, utter helplessness and rage. Anger was a new experience to him. The student's awe of the counselor diminished and his self-reliance increased; he began to sense the futility of his dependency and the extent of his demands. When, during the spring vacation, he had a chance to observe himself with his family, his perception of his father changed radically: he saw him now as a rather passive man wrestling with his own inner problems. The student was able to complete his academic work and later to act on his decision to enter therapy.

A girl who was early frightened into submission and emotional bluntness by her parents' uncontrolled punishing became aware of her feelings towards them only after having reenacted with the counselor an episode that had recurred with her mother; provoking an attack through sullen passivity, feeling panicky, angry and guilty, and returning to propitiate the attacker by promises and apologies. The intensity of her feelings, and their lack of "fit" to the actual incident with the counselor, made vivid to her the early context in which these feelings had originated and led to first hesitant attempts at direct self-assertion with her parents.

Clarification of significant patterns in the transference plays an important role only in the counseling of students with neurotic personality structures. The majority of those who struggle with normal adolescent problems tend to work on their relationship to parents directly, making maximum use of their current experiences in the family. For the latter a clarification of obviously transferred reactions represents only a contributory source of insight. This clarification, together with the venting of realistic

Specific Features of Therapeutic Work

complaints, serves mainly to keep clear the path of communication between student and counselor.

We have described so far the students' genuine attempts to integrate their current experiences in the family with the insights gained in counseling and to use them to achieve a more mature relationship with the parents. From these productive struggles one must distinguish the episodic attempts to use counseling to control or to hurt parents, which leave intact the structure of the existing relationship. These attempts take a different shape in the different stages of counseling; they will be described in chronological sequence.

Usually the student will tell the parents about being in counseling at the time when he feels at least partially ready to handle the conversation productively in the context of on-going attempts at communication and change. The time chosen depends both on his progress and on his estimate of the parents' ability to assimilate the news. This estimate may be grossly erroneous; witness the case of a student who felt that his unsuspecting parents must be protected from the shock, while they, in fact, did not dare to broach to him the issue of getting help and were calling the Center for advice. But if the student immediately tells the news to parents who actually deny the existence of problems, or view the need of help as a sign of abnormality, his intent is questionable. The shocked and worried parents may accede to the demands they have resisted, or try to bear with behavior they cannot understand or accept. Such forced change seldom lasts and it contributes nothing to a real resolution of the conflict. Sometimes an interaction of this kind forms the main content of the pre-counseling period. Once the student has learned what counseling is all about and has realized that his intent in coming has been to change the parents, he is faced with having to decide between leaving or entering counseling.

Later on, opportunities for controlling parents are presented by discussions of the counseling experiences with them. In contrast to actively working out with them an insight derived from counseling, the student may simply tell the parents of what had gone on in sessions, or of what the counselor had said. This course may be rationalized by a reference to some general maxim: "Parents must know what bothers their children," "It is good to share"; yet it often reflects a thinly disguised wish to retaliate or inflict hurt on the parent without taking the responsibility for this action, a "see what you've done to me" attitude. The "sharing" may also reflect a student's inability to separate himself from his parents and serve to perpetuate his dependency. To feel convinced himself, he must first convince them, must be granted what he ambivalently wants without having to claim it: "If my mother realizes that she is keeping me dependent, she'll give me my freedom." If dependent-rebellious attitudes are maintained towards both the parents and the counselor the student may try to pit them against each other and place himself as a passive bystander, quoting one to another and giving his alliance to each in turn. The counselor must be careful not to lend himself to such use, which permits the student to avoid facing his own conflict by externalizing it, with roles distributed between the parent and the counselor.

In the cases of those students for whom counseling serves as an introduction to outside therapy, the parents' attitude to this plan, as well as the student's feelings about seeking their help, must be assessed during the year. If there is entrenched hostility toward the parents, or if the student is aware of his wish to exploit them, or feels a strong need to make therapy his own unaided enterprise, he may decide against private therapy. Students who apply to outpatient clinics, either for these reasons or because of the family's lack of funds, can do so without involving the parents. The majority of the well-to-do approach the parents eventually. The task of obtaining their support, or of arriving at the decision to forego it, usually falls into a late stage of the counseling period. This task presents pitfalls of its own.

If the parents have had clear evidence of the student's progress in counseling they are usually glad to support therapy if they can afford it. When such evidence is missing, or misperceived, or when the parents feel strongly about the stigma attached to psychiatric treatment, or about the expenses involved, the student is faced with a difficult problem. In this situation he may once more feel in need of support and may want the counselor to plead his case with the parents. Justifiable as this wish appears, the insistence on it often covers up the student's own unresolved conflicts about further therapy. If the counselor undertakes to convince the parents he may find that once he succeeds the student himself loses interest in the plan. In most of our cases willingness to approach the parents on one's own is one of the criteria of the student's readiness for therapy. He may have fleeting fantasies about the counselor doing the persuading but will not actually ask for assistance; he may feel relieved, however, if the counselor is willing to back him up in case of need.

Once the student is ready to face the parents in earnest he often finds them much more receptive than he had expected, or than they had been before. If he has to go through a hard struggle to secure their help, or even fails to obtain it, he still gains insight and self-confidence in the process; the same is true if he arrives at a decision to forego the parents' support realizing that, in his particular circumstances, this support might make therapy less effective.

> The father of a girl who was much afraid of hurting and disillusioning her parents reluctantly agreed to pay for her therapy, but when the first bill arrived explosively refused to do so, maintaining that she had misunderstood him. The student returned to the counselor, and after facing her own

suppressed fury, was able for the first time to confront her father with her disappointment and anger. Another student in a similar situation met the parents' challenge that he himself pay for the therapy by finding a job at the school and borrowing a sum of money from a friend.

In all these cases the counselor's well-intentioned intervention would have deprived the student of an opportunity for personal growth and for working out some of his problems with his parents. The situation is different in cases of acute breakdowns, in some borderline cases, or in cases where the parents themselves are severely disturbed. The intervention necessary in these cases can be best handled by the college psychiatrist.

Occasionally the counselor finds himself wrestling not only with the student's images of the parents, but with the parents themselves: they may call, write, or visit the counselor. Some students wish the counselor to see the parent, or support the parent's wish for a meeting, either for the reasons discussed above or for some others: the student may hope, for instance, that the meeting will magically clarify his image of the parent. The motives underlying the wish are usually close to awareness, and more often than not the discussion of such requests leads to their withdrawal. If both student and parent persist, the purpose and the conditions of the meeting must be clarified in advance; it must be understood that the counselor will not divulge any confidential information about the student, and that he has the right to tell the student about the content of the exchange. Sometimes the student's motives for sponsoring the contact can be clarified only after the meeting has taken place. Apart from this, our experience has shown the value of such meetings to be negligible.

When the parents initiate the contact, often without the students' knowledge, they are usually prompted by anxiety, and wish to find out what is wrong with their son or daughter and how they should act to be helpful. These specific wishes cannot as a rule be fulfilled, but the parents' anxiety and guilt feelings can often be allayed by a general discussion of the problems of adolescence, or by direct or implied reassurance. When this seems insufficient the parent may be made aware of the possibility of discussing his concerns with some expert outside the Center. The rare parents who appear at the Center unannounced may be referred to other school offices for a discussion of the student's academic or other manifest problems. If they insist on a confidential talk they may be given the opportunity to speak to a counselor on the Center's staff other than the one who works with the student. This opportunity has been used by some parents for discussing their own personal problems.

Exceptional events will occur. One father presented to the counselor a systematic case against his daughter, well documented with photostatic evidence. An irate couple came to demand that the counselor stop their daughter from keeping company with a boy of a different religion. A persistent father's intent in meeting the counselor was to discredit his ability and judgment in his son's eyes. Another father threatened the counselor with legal prosecution for withholding information on his daughter. Others have been more subtle, and have had their family physicians request personal data on the student. The majority of the parents, however, accept the rule of confidentiality once the reasons have been explained to them and are receptive to the idea conveyed by most of our comments: that counseling as well as the total process of growing up is inevitably the adolescent's own enterprise.

B. *School Authorities*

Faculty members and administrative officers are often cast as surrogate figures, sometimes consciously, sometimes unconsciously. Within such relationships the counselor can sometimes guide students toward reintegrative experiences similar to those involving family members. Genetic insight may be central in the corrective influence of such experiences, or it may be peripheral.

An example of the former is the case of a boy who had indiscriminately rejected his father as a masculine failure only to bolster his own weakened sense of adequacy by just as indiscriminately idolizing a series of teachers. Each of these suffered the father's fate in the boy's eyes when they inevitably showed indications of less than heroic qualities. Eventually he traced this pattern to his early years during the war when his image of a father was of a mythic figure who appeared mysteriously at unpredictable intervals only to leave him repeatedly to the less glorious but more trustworthy care of his mother. He came to see the repetitive pattern of the present as serving primarily to preserve the mythic father image and to cause periodic retreats to feminine identification figures. With this insight he began to establish a more satisfying relationship at home and to entertain new possibilities in relationships with his teachers who remained more realistic identity-testing figures than the father.

An example of the *peripheral* influence of genetic insight in such re-educative experiences is the case of a girl who could not participate in class discussions, and risked failures in her courses rather than seek the guidance of individual conferences with her teachers. Covert expectations of ridicule and rejection were traced to childhood experiences, with no visible therapeutic gain. The same expectations were found in the transference, but again with no consequent movement. In the midst of an academic crisis a conference with one of her teachers, dramatically planned in the counseling sessions, brought the unrealistic nature of her expectations so clearly into focus that she began to face seriously for the first time her own self-defeating tendencies.

Simply to have encouraged this girl to put her fears to a test would of course have been futile had it not followed the preparation described. It is notable, however, that when the break came it did so by way of a parent-surrogate relationship in the immediate present, without explicit reference to its prototype.

The altered roles that authority and dependency can assume in a young person's outlook as a consequence of moving from home to college are not only important for the reorienting of old attitudes but also for the orienting of new ones. At this age past identifications are naturally being reviewed and tested for their capacity to support a sense of personal identity and social competence. Thus teachers, deans, etc. have an intrinsic appeal as catalytic *foci* for the testing of new defensive and expressive skills. This sometimes poses the question to the counselor, in respect to a given student-teacher relationship, of whether it holds more promise for the deepening of insight or, as it were, for the extending of out-sight, i.e., whether it seems to lend itself more aptly to un-learning or to just plain learning. The discontinuity of academic relationships does not always allow for both.

An extremely bright, docile, self-effacing girl who suffered from periodic severe attacks of insomnia had reached the point in counseling where freshly emergent adequacy feelings resulted in behavior which for a time seemed arrogant to some who had known her previously. A teacher, with whom she had been working on a special project and whose recommendation she needed for a Fulbright scholarship, began to complain that she was no longer the personable young lady she had been when he had taken an interest in her — he even suggested that she think of counseling! A crisis came when she felt she had to choose between the Fulbright and "reverting to my old frightened ways." It seemed to the counselor a particularly harsh choice. There were features in the relationship that could have been used to show the crisis as a partial displacement of transference feelings, perhaps averting thereby her inclination to forego the scholarship in the exercise of her new convictions. However, her ability to make this choice at a time when she was particularly mobilized for important personality change promised to have a more neutralizing influence on an underlying hostile-dependent character pattern than further insight might have exerted.

It will be seen from the above that the college counselor functions in a particularly fluid therapeutic situation. Typically the non-college therapist attempts to draw the transference into the therapy sessions and to seek corrective emotional experiences there. In so doing he grows accustomed to a sense of relatively direct control in matters relating to transference and counter-transference. In college counseling much of the relevant transference and counter-transference is spread over a range of relationships, the counseling sessions serving as a kind of pivotal clearing house for misperceptions of both kinds. In this position the counselor does well to develop a sense of confidence in the remote control that resides in the counseling relationship.

Appreciation of resultant advantages and disadvantages is therefore in order. One advantage stems from the fact that in the college age group seemingly routine choices often represent turning points of dynamic significance. The counselor's vantage point thus affords him occasional opportunities to relate himself to the deeper implications of choice situations, which to the authorities involved must appear superficial.

A girl had committed herself in early adolescence to the ascetic life of a book-worm. She entered counseling after several encounters with boys had awakened feminine desires, only to precipitate a depressing sense of "artificiality." It developed she possessed artistic talents, which she indulged at painfully infrequent intervals. Most of her energy she devoted to maintaining a mediocre record as a physics major, which not only left her little time for art but now represented an obstacle to increasingly pressing social impulses. The obvious decision to switch her major from physics to art came in the middle of a semester, which forced her to choose between postponing a strongly motivated act of personal emancipation and confronting her family and professors with her intention to fail a course for the first time in her life. She openly appreciated that an emotional commitment to her femininity was at stake. Unconsciously, however, the choice challenged her ability to channel homosexual as well as heterosexual impulses. This had only been touched on in an early session when she recounted memories of believing she could be a boy and the bitterness with which she ultimately resigned herself to girlhood. Thus the counselor saw in the prospect of this girl's active failing of physics, in order to make a positive feminine commitment, an opportunity for her to establish a more liberal mastery over threatening unconscious impulses. And, it seemed, if she waited for time to soften the choice this dynamic leverage might have worn thin. With the counselor's support she chose to invite the failure, thus initiating a series of enriching experiences.

The possibility of utilizing relatively routine situations to such rich advantage carries with it the disadvantage of tempting the counselor into advising or other non-therapeutic roles. The strategy involved is similar to that of the parleyed long shot, and indeed, an element of gambling is very much present. As the successful gambler knows, in such ventures preparation, discrimination, and timing are essential. The cardinal therapeutic rule of not taking sides lest the patient's freedom of expression be subtly restricted must have long been observed prior to the strategic move, and the counselor should have substantial evidence of the student's readiness to carry the move through on his own resources.

In some cases a diversified transference can bring feelings into the open that might not otherwise see the light of day in short term treatment.

> A girl began counseling rather exaggeratedly fearing dramatic sexual pathologies. As if to qualify as a *bona fide* patient she quickly aspired to an affair with the counselor. Having thus committed herself to what she considered an advanced psychosexual level she could not admit to less sophisticated feelings. After ten sessions the counselor was surprised to learn through official channels that this girl was on academic probation. In a subsequent session an offhand inquiry into her academic status brought an outburst of tears and then the information that she had just come from the Dean's office where her fears met such kindness that she "just bawled like a baby for the first time in front of someone." She then revealed previously suppressed feelings of being totally insignificant, and the sexual fantasies were approachable from this perspective.

A disadvantage is the rare case where the transference in the counseling relationship is so diluted by an investment of it elsewhere as to be rendered ineffective. This may happen, for example, if the student remains emotionally attached to the teacher to whom he first spoke about his personal problems and who subsequently referred him to the Counseling Center.

One of the more delicate aspects of the counselor's pivotal position in relation to diversified transference is the unpredictability of the counter-transference. In most instances, if the counselor has seen to it that the student's feelings and anticipations have been adequately explored, any spontaneous pattern of response from the surrogate figure can be expected to have clarifying effects; all things considered, college faculties include a number of mature people. On infrequent occasions, however, counter-transferences are met which have the effect of reinforcing a student's unhealthy expectations.

A many-faceted feature of college counseling presents itself at this point: the surrogate figure is very often a personal friend or working colleague of the counselor. This has the advantage of enabling the counselor to call on his own observations in understanding surrogate relationships and not to depend solely on the client's point of view as most therapists must do. He may know Professor Doe, for example, to be eminently reasonable in face-to-face contacts and extremely generous with his time, although the student's impression of him as unyielding and abrupt may be justified on the basis of classroom observations alone.

On the other hand, the counselor's known or speculated friendship for this or that colleague may have the effect of discouraging optimal candor in the sessions of some students despite the confidentiality agreement. It is of course difficult to assess the extent of this drawback; however, a number of disarming experiences has suggested that we look for such reluctance more often than is warranted.

Chance over-lunch or cocktail hints and clues as to how a given colleague currently perceives a given client in an approaching crisis between the two can sensitize the counselor's timing and tactical handling of the crisis when it comes. Information of this nature is fortuitous, and yet the number of such coincidences suggests that some colleagues tip the counselors off on the chance that one of them is working with a certain student.

If it seems of therapeutic advantage to the student the counselor can make such exchange of information open and mutual, after exploring the pros and contras of doing so with the student, and after receiving his permission. Especially in cases of necessary severance from school the counselor may in this way initiate a chain of events that turns a punitive situation into one of cooperative reflection and planning. Such cooperative ventures have resulted in a few fertile opportunities for mutual education between the counseling and administrative staffs with regard to their respective contribution to the meeting of commonly held responsibilities.

The counselor, typically working as he does in a confidential atmosphere of mutual introspection with one student at a time, tends to lose sight of the constructive effects to be sought in the decisive exercise of authority. An occasional putting together of heads with a talented and experienced dean can remind him that merely understanding a person does not exhaust the possibilities of helping him. The Dean on his part deals routinely with students in overt trouble, for whom he is typically cast as a negative person. There can be in such day-to-day contacts a subtly erosive influence on his professional posture. Irrational and immature behavior comes to be taken personally, rather than as the materials of his special craft. The counselor's trained reflex of thinking always in terms of the history of behavior, reinforced daily as it is by witnessing a wider range of transference phenomena, makes him less subject to this influence, and his immunity in this regard has been noticed to rub off on his administrative colleagues with visibly lasting effect.

The professional advantages of the counselor's position on a small campus come with some disadvantages for his personal relationships. The social mores of an educational institution unmistakably define the channel of privileged communication as between staff member and staff member. There are sound reasons for this, as there are for its prototype: the privileged communication between parent and parent. The confidentiality agreement of psychological counseling is therefore alien to the fabric of tacit values and expectations that stabilizes the working *esprit de corps* of educators. Plausible though it is, when one reflects on it, to make the counseling service the one institutionalized exception to this set of mores, it is not without consequence that it is plausible *only* when one reflects on it. Suppressed hostility, suspiciousness, grudging cooperation and outright interference should be expected periodically from colleagues with whom one otherwise enjoys relationships of mutual respect and affection. For the counselor this is an occupational fact of life, to be lived with at as small cost to personal pleasure as possible. He can never be sure, however, that his skill in blending responsibility and personability has met all possible contingencies. A new challenge may come in a phone call from a beginner at the Office of Student Personnel or the Infirmary, or in a department or faculty meeting, or in the midst of a campus crisis when the exception to the established channel of privileged communication feels particularly out of place, or over a friendly beer at the local bar. In particularly awkward situations the temptation is strong to stretch a point and include someone in the definition of "professional confidence" that the counselor well knows the student would not agree was included. Such situations are best governed by a rule that when the counselor must choose between making light of his confidentiality agreements and appearing to his colleagues unduly officious, unfriendly, stuffy, or odd he should always choose the latter. An effective counseling service in a community as compact as a college campus is not otherwise possible.

Finally, it remains a fact of reality that the counselor *is* a university official, however clear the agreement may be that establishes a special relationship with his clients. Three sets of problems follow, some of which were mentioned in passing:

when the counselor also teaches certain courses which it would be an academic hardship for a student to forego, and arrangements cannot be made with another counselor, we have found it a workable compromise to insist that the period of counseling either precede or follow the course. We have learned through making exceptions to this procedure that while the course work seems to have no untoward effect on the counseling, and may even enrich it from the point of view of resolving transference attitudes, the counseling has unpredictable effects on the course work. One student was unable to complete written assignments for the first six weeks of a semester due to misplaced resistance. He eventually worked it through but by then the course was practically a total loss to him. Even when the course work is not directly impaired the necessity of assigning grades to clients creates a sticky problem. A "B", for example, comes unconsciously to mean not only that one *was* a "B" *student* in Psychology 15a, say, but that one *is* a grade "B" *person*. This problem is best solved by avoiding it.

Secondly, letters of recommendation create a problem. As a rule it is best to decline such requests from present or former clients, investigating perhaps their reluctance to rely on the judgments of teachers who know their academic work at a closer range. It is true for a significant minority of students, however, even in a small college, that after four years there is no one professor who can write more than a sterile variation on a theme already represented by an uninformative grade point average. Consequently, the counselor may sometimes not only render an additional valid service to a student but also make available to some known or unknown admissions committee that which it most prizes, a really discriminating appraisal of the candidate. Whether and when to comply with such requests should be governed by considerations that vary from case to case. By agreeing to write a letter for a boy with divorced parents the counselor inadvertently passed the test of whether he himself could adjust conflicting loyalties, with the result that the boy came to see this as the issue central to his problems.

In the case of one girl a recurrent form of resistance was employed in order to gain the counselor's esteem, with the result that each new prospect of unfolding her considerable repertoire of "badnesses" brought with it the temptation to quit while she might still be ahead. One such period of resistance was punctuated by a request for a letter of recommendation. The counselor replied that if he could ever write such a letter it would probably be a favorable one but that, as she knew, her therapy could not afford his recording anything favorable about her until she came to terms with her own inevitable private reservations. There followed a helpful account, long suppressed, of other ways in which she felt herself to be hopelessly neurotic.

In a case representing a counterpart of the last, a girl, after the end of therapy, revealed the extent of the changes that had taken place by willingly reading the counselor's letter of recommendation and accepting its favorable content as a plain statement of truth. In the past she never believed anything complimentary to herself and had been so afraid of finding out what people really felt about her that she would lose the papers returned to her by her teachers so as not to have to read their comments.

Finally, as a university official, the counselor tends to share the high value placed by educators on uninterrupted academic achievement. Thus there is the occasional danger of not appreciating those cases in which therapeutic progress must be accompanied by academic lapses. The three of us religiously study each issue of the probation and Dean's lists, ostensibly to keep informed on matters of probable importance to clients. Actually what is involved is a kind of self-reassuring solitaire by which we keep track of the number of cases, unknown to any but ourselves, in which therapeutic progress is accompanied by academic distinction, against the number of cases in which it is accompanied by academic failure. Since the students in the latter category far more frequently make known their status as patients the counseling staff are not strangers to narcissistic frustration — which probably accounts for the unusual interest with which we follow the academic score.

C. *Peers*

Participation of the student's friends in the counseling process is often limited to its initial period: as he himself obtains firsthand experience the importance of the opinion of others decreases. Nevertheless, for all but the isolates, some sharing of this new experience is a rule; usually it is limited to intimates, but it may also include a wide range of acquaintances. If two or more friends are simultaneously seen at the Center, the emotional significance of this exchange is greatly enhanced: the vivid experiencing of the presence and the claims of others refutes the fantasy of an exclusive possession of the counselor. This situation tends to evoke feelings pertaining to sibling relationships and to the parents' attitudes toward siblings, underlining the family-like features of the counseling set-up.

As in the case of multiple authority figures the special transference relationships that result have both advantages and drawbacks. Feelings about siblings which might have remained dormant may be vividly experienced and worked out in this situation and new attitudes to age-equals formed. Yet suspicion that the counselor knows the friends on whom conflicting feelings become focused may make the student curb free expression, lest the situation between him and the counselor become too real and personal. For example, if the counselor is known to work with a friend the student may be afraid that the counselor prefers the friend and would be personally annoyed by an expression of hostility towards him, as he would not be by a report of a real sibling rivalry. Thus a girl tried to control her wish to disparage her rival in a theatrical performance who had previously worked with the same counselor. A common defense against a fear of the situation becoming too personal is to reject counseling as being "too impersonal," so there is no call to open up! "There are so many of us, and our problems so similar, you could not possibly be interested in each, I am just a case."

Whereas alertness to the student's unexpressed or disguised feelings about "the others" is the prime requisite, two general conditions must be fulfilled to insure the optimal utilization of the situation. Each student must be given the certainty that his therapy is his own; even though he himself may choose to share some of it with friends the counselor does not follow suit: he will not discuss a counseled student with an involved or worried friend. Second, the counselor must take care not to provide any basis for intensified rivalry, keeping in mind that notes are constantly being compared. ("My friend came last week with a similar problem — and you didn't tell *him* to wait till fall!") To avoid what could seem as favoritism we decline requests of some students to continue as private patients after their allowance of counseling time is expended, although this refusal often involves frustration on both sides. We also discourage students from planning to work in counseling from midyear to midyear after having observed the reaction of some to being "dropped" while their friends continue through the year. In this matter as in that of providing additional sessions we will depart from equality in favor of individual need, but not without considering the possible reverberations of each departure.

Within this framework discussion of one's therapeutic experiences can benefit both the counseled student and his friends. Student bull sessions in which views on problematic life issues are exchanged often become chaotic or sterile; an injection of some genuine personal insight may give them a new direction and vigor. The student who shares with others an insight gained in counseling has a chance to test its general validity and to discover individual variations. Thus the interlinking of counseling with informal group discussions usually has a stimulating and stabilizing effect on both processes.

Friends or roommates will usually exchange therapeutic insights. Where there is friction the student at some point gets ready to vent his grudges; if he knows that the other is in counseling also, reliance on the friend's growing insight helps him to overcome the fear of hurting or alienating him. A crisis handled by both in a new way is a greatly encouraging experience.

In some rare cases a friend is used as a subsidiary therapist, with good results. One girl's most vital therapeutic experiences were released by regular talks with a friend who was well advanced in her own analysis. Typically, feelings and thoughts pushed away in the counseling session returned and struck with full force after a review with the friend, and their implications were worked on in the following session. More often such use of a friend is slight and episodic, but the anxiety-allaying effect of sharing some "guilty secret" with an age-equal is observed fairly frequently. Thus a boy who was deeply ashamed of what he considered perverse sexual feelings became markedly more willing to work on them in the counseling sessions after having admitted them to another whom he suspected of being similarly afflicted; as a side result the other student was encouraged to apply for counseling also.

In less favorable constellations of internal and external circumstances exchange with friends may over-dilute or confuse

Specific Features of Therapeutic Work

the therapeutic experience and deprive it of its personal focusing. Often it serves to maintain some neurotic pattern of relationships: stories about counseling, or mutual analyses, are used for prestige, dominance, expression of hostility, etc. In some exceptional cases such misuse is deliberate. One student had a standing appointment with his blasé crowd after each session delighting them with reports of his clever repartees, and of how he was gradually "breaking down the counselor."

Much more frequent is the situation that occurs when two or more disturbed students form an alliance from which they obtain for a time some intense satisfactions, ambivalent as they may be. At the least, a group of this kind — of which we encountered more among girls than among boys — permits the members some freedom of expression, even if mutual tolerance is forced and grudging: "I listen to her complaints because then she has to listen to mine; she isn't really sympathetic, but at least she lets me talk." If a member of such a need-connected group enters counseling the precarious group balance is threatened. In this case psychological discussions stimulated by counseling tend to be unconsciously used to preserve the existing relationship patterns in a new guise, and therapy makes slow progress; it may even be given up by the student who believes that this newly found "group therapy" is a much richer source of insights. The feeling that counseling conflicts with group discussion, and that the content of the latter must be kept from the counselor, is an earmark of those instances of "group work" in which the neurotic aspects predominate over the truly exploratory. The counselor, however, does well not to press the issue prematurely: a doubtful or untimely "clarification" may intensify the student's conflict between therapy and "therapeutic friendship" at a time when few other social satisfactions are yet available. Problems involved in counseling members of a clique are exemplified by the following case:

A group of disturbed girls who had chosen to live together in a small dormitory and were causing troubles to the resident counselor were advised by her to seek help. The majority took the advice and several of them had to be seen by the same counselor. The first to come was one of the dominant girls of the group; like the other two leaders she was gifted, artistic, and given to dramatic enactment of her fantasies. She made productive use of counseling, working intensively on her feelings towards her family (including intense rivalry with a married sister) and her attitudes towards men. Both she and the other group members who came later and were clearly the followers and the underdogs touched only lightly on the current events in the dormitory. After achieving a substantial improvement in her relationship to her family and her boy friend this girl developed a strong automatic resistance to any communication in the sessions, until her days were spent in a futile struggle to break through that wall. Finally she accepted the counselor's suggestion that she stop struggling and save her allotment of sessions for later, and left with relief. In the following years she came for brief but productive periods of counseling centered around her progress reports. This girl fared better in counseling than the "followers" who were hesitant and cautious in sessions and most of whom discontinued without having made much progress.

The only girl who stayed in counseling for the full term and got full benefit from it occupied a position between the in- and the out-group which, as she soon realized, reflected her own inner conflicts. Unlike the others she responded to the pointers about her avoiding to touch on the group issues, but started discussing them only after the other girls had stopped coming. She formed new friendships during this period and withdrew from the dormitory group before it was dissolved by administrative action at the end of the year.

From hints jointly contributed by group members and from later chance information it became clear that the girls in the "inner circle" not only fascinated others by their discussion of psychological dynamics and by the dramatic episodes they created, but were also greatly resented for their dominance. They were also held guilty of "stealing boys" from the others and then speedily dropping them; therefore giving the whole group a black mark. Obviously both the offender and the offended held back from venting their feelings on the issue for fear of endangering their standing both with the counselor and with each other.

Had it been feasible to have a separate counselor for each girl the difficulty might have been avoided. For a group all members of which would accept counseling mainly with a view to improving their common situation, group counseling might be preferable to individual work with the same counselor, might in fact be a method of choice.

This case suggests also that it pays to look for some interpersonal complications at the basis of those episodes of strong resistance that seem out of line with the student's personality and his attitude towards the counselor.

A senior girl in applying for counseling with a particular staff member concealed the identity of her fiancé, who was formerly seen by this counselor and advised to seek treatment. She presented her engagement as unproblematic and concentrated on her feelings towards her family; gradually she became more acceptant of them and was able to introduce her fiancé and obtain the parents' agreement to an early marriage. After that her productions in sessions became vague and repetitive, and the counselor's comments precipitated an inner conflict about stopping or moving ahead. This conflict was solved as if by a *deus ex machina* when at a student party the counselor became aware of the identity of the fiancé. The girl then confessed her panic about her impending marriage to a man who — as both she and the counselor knew — was not ready for a real commitment. She accepted a referral to a private therapist with whom she could continue after graduation, while her fiancé also made plans for therapy. Marriage was postponed and took place a year later.

This girl's conscious reason for concealment was the fear that if the truth were known she would be assigned to a different counselor, but this very determination to work with one who knew her boy friend sprang from her conflict about her marriage plans. Since she knew that chances of being "found out" were high, and practically invited discovery on the given occasion, it seems likely that she had wished for just this outcome: her misgivings came to light without her having been guilty of any disloyalty toward the boy.

It happens occasionally that a girl, after having made a good start in counseling, slows down or stops working in sessions as soon as a relationship with a boy has been established or mended, yet shows no wish to stop coming; the counselor is cast in the role of a confidante who must listen and sympathize. This behavior may reflect merely the girl's need for support, or pleasure in sharing, and end when her confidence in the new relationship has become secure, which may also end counseling. However, if the affair is obviously unhappy and fraught with internal conflict, and yet every comment except reassurance is persistently denounced by the girl as devaluating her tie to the boy, the situation must not be permitted to drag. Its clarification including a review of antecedents either removes obstacles to movement or precipitates a decision to discontinue counseling. A student who makes this decision with some insight into her motives is likely to resume counseling if and when experience proves to her the futility of her hope that all her problems can be solved through a given relationship.

Sharing a counselor with a friend can cause complications in cases of intense relationships and is best avoided when possible. The students' wish to work with a therapist who did well with a friend is a common occurrence, and so are referrals of friends to one's former counselor. The wish to bring a friend to the counselor one is still working with is less frequent and is rarely simple.

> A student who repeatedly became part of a triangle of girl-friends and then acted to disrupt it, succeeded in steering a very disturbed girl to her woman counselor. She had rarely mentioned this girl and felt the relationship to be of no importance. Yet the fantasies she brought out after her counselor had passed this girl to another, made it likely that she would have left in dejection and anger if the counselor were to have worked with the friend without letting her in on this work or showing in some way that theirs was the primary alliance.

When sharing of a counselor occurs accidentally, with no personal motives involved, it is usually possible to reduce the difficulties by pointing them out to each student. Thus two incompatible roommates, each seeking counseling for reasons unrelated to the other and later discovering that they see the same counselor, can be made aware that this discovery has resulted in a lesser freedom of expression. In the beginning stage one of the two may be willing to change therapists; if the work is well under way both will usually prefer to continue, attempting to keep alert to their feelings concerning each other. If they succeed counseling proceeds without hindrance and may even lead to a speedier resolution of mutual conflicts. On the other hand the interpersonal situation created by sharing a counselor may happen to reproduce a significant pattern which is a focus of disturbance for one or both students. In this case the situation is much more difficult, but occasionally it can also be used to much greater advantage. Its optimal utilization sometimes requires a departure from the established routines.

> Two girls entered counseling knowing each other only slightly, but later they formed a strong tie marked both by rivalry and mutual dependence. Both were older sisters and had been more than usually traumatized by the arrival of a sibling. At the time when one of them re-entered counseling after a planned interruption, conflicts between them were on the increase, but they glossed over any misgivings they might have had about working with the same counselor. Both girls soon gave evidence of covert preoccupation with the issue of their "counseling seniority" and the fear of putting it to a test led to a merely token involvement in therapy. Only after the counselor provided a "test" of who would "yield the field" and provoked an emotional storm by suggesting to each that she reconsider the "joint" arrangement, did they realize that the issue of rivalry had not been solved by quick insight and subsequent forgetting. That the students were treated equally in this incident was probably essential to its resolution; moreover, their "counseling status" was actually identical: each had had a period of separate work with the counselor and had built up some confidence in the relationship.
> When the counselor received contradictory reports from the two girls (the facts in question bearing on their respective claims on the counselor) she asked each for permission to quote her report to the other. This request was misinterpreted as intending a general breaking of confidentiality; the

dreams depicted being forced to admit the other into one's own sessions. Much confusion had to be worked through before each girl discovered the rich admixture of fantasy in her own perceptions as well as in those of the friend. By the time of termination their images of each other were much more realistic and the intensity of their relationship had lessened.

The total course of counseling in this case was punctuated by episodes of strong emotions each resulting in a period of productive work. Most of them were precipitated by experiences with the therapist and/or with the friend and some were vividly identified with episodes from childhood; thus the fear one girl felt at a college function of being noticed and judged by the counselor revived the early frustrated wish to have her mother leave the baby to come and watch her perform at a party. These episodes of intense emotions served both to make the genetic insights alive and real and to increase the awareness of the current everyday feelings; both students made marked progress during the term of sharing the counselor. The therapist's remarks and actions were used alternately as a focus of fantasies and as a bridge to reality, and she had to watch herself closely so as not to foster confusion.

Simultaneous work by the same counselor with two persons who are intensely involved with each other is fraught with risks because of intensified complex transference which makes stringent demands on the therapist's self-awareness and acumen. For the same reason this arrangement can, under favorable conditions, invigorate and speed up the therapeutic process, and might even be the method of choice in some interpersonal situations. In college counseling, however, this method has no place, because the set time limit does not permit an adequate working out and resolution of transference.

4. Termination

In the section on the pre-counseling period we discussed the cases of students who drop out — temporarily or permanently — without having entered counseling in earnest. The present section deals with termination of counseling after it has been entered and pursued for a period of time.

The feature of the college set-up that bears most directly on the shaping of this end-stage is the *predetermined limit* to the period of continuous counseling, a limit of which the students are informed in advance. As a rule it is set at the end of the academic year, when the majority of students leave the area to pursue their various summer plans. This timing permits the student to leave the counselor rather than feel that he is being dropped; it mitigates the arbitrariness of termination and is much preferable to enforcing a stop during the academic year when it can easily arouse resentment in the student and guilt feelings in the counselor. The time limit is a necessary consequence of the relation of the available staff time to the students' demand for counseling, and is usually accepted by them as insuring a fair chance to all. Within these necessary limits termination in a college set-up can still be handled flexibly: it need be neither absolute nor abrupt when both the student and the counselor remain on campus. Students who discontinue counseling — either by choice, or at the end of the year — without having used up their quota of time (the length of the academic year) may be given the option of resuming it at some later date. Any student can return for a few additional sessions when the counselor has time available, or keep in touch through occasional visits. Many students who terminate counseling in the spring visit the counselor in the fall to tell of their summer experiences or to discuss further plans.

The existence of the time limit affects but little those students who complete counseling to their satisfaction in the course of the academic year, or terminate for other reasons, sometimes well in advance of the deadline. Such termination can be simple and smooth, or it can be an enactment of the struggle for emancipation. This struggle may lead to a premature termination, but more often the dependence-independence dilemma is reflected in the uncertainty the students harbor about their readiness to leave counseling. Thus a student, after having reached the satisfying decision to live away from home after graduation, may now demand reassurance from the counselor that he is ready to leave counseling; the next week he may decisively assert his independence and confidently stride out of the room.

The struggle for emancipation from counseling may also reveal to the student, sometimes in a dramatic fashion, the specific pattern involved in his or her dependence on parents.

A girl who was very happy about what had been achieved in counseling spent several sessions inconclusively weighing pros and contras of terminating. The counselor finally communicated to the student her impression, that though not sure of her reasons, she really wanted to leave, and wondered why she could not just act on this wish; she could always return if she wanted. The student after a moment of silence exclaimed with smiles and tears that she just realized that this was what she had always wanted her mother to say to her. She was then able to express the feelings that had been an obstacle to leaving the counselor: "We come here one after another with our problems and miseries, and when we leave happy — what reward do *you* get for the trouble you took? It isn't fair to you!" She left this last session with the feeling that her growing up would not leave her parents without any reward, nor herself without any affectionate ties to the family.

A standstill in counseling after a period of successful work is often an indication of a conflict about a wish to leave, but this wish itself may stem from different sources. If it reflects the student's unwillingness to explore a problem that next presents itself, he may leave on an impulse, avoiding a discussion of his reasons; this may also happen in response to some false move or failure of understanding on the part of the counselor. However, some exploration of the wish to leave is usually possible, and even students who leave abruptly will often accept the invitation to return for a concluding session. If the obstacles to continuation can be identified they may be overcome in the process; if they prove too strong the student may make a more conscious and responsible decision to leave counseling — at least for the time being.

In the instances of termination discussed so far the existence of a fixed time limit affects the events only indirectly and slightly. The student's internal struggle for emancipation may be speeded up by the knowledge of the limit, and the counselor's tempo and decisions are often influenced by it. For those who see the end of the year approach without having achieved certainty that their current problems have been largely resolved termination has varied significance. Its approach often precipitates conscious attempts to evaluate the progress made and some less conscious testing of one's readiness to leave. Some feelings about separation from the counselor are usually present, even if there has been no marked transference and if the student is satisfied with his gains. His willingness to explore and acknowledge those feelings presages more readiness to be on one's own than does denial. One girl in leaving counseling shortly before the time limit, though teary-eyed, strongly denied any regrets: "I don't feel guilty about leaving you, nor dependent, nor rejected. Maybe you want me to say I care for you and will miss you; besides," she smiled, "somehow I have the feeling that this isn't goodbye. I think I'll see you around somewhere." And she did,

Specific Features of Therapeutic Work

in the counselor's room the following year. An exploration of the student's feelings and fantasies concerning separation bring him a step closer to an inner acceptance of termination.

As a rule a certain tapering-off of self-exploration takes place towards the end of the counseling period, and the advent of the final examinations often leads to a decision to terminate. However, many of the students who have moved rapidly in counseling continue to work with unabated energy to the end, the last sessions being as probing and exploratory as the earlier ones. The counselors need not feel uneasy about new areas being opened up by these students even in the last session: reports given by them after the summer vacations often show not only a consolidation of the gains previously made but also a rapid movement towards a resolution of issues that have been barely if at all touched upon. Potential for growth at this age must not be underestimated, and the student is often right when he postpones to the fall the assessment of his gains, and of his need for further therapy.

For some of the students whose neurotic problems are fairly severe the issue of termination and of subsequent referral is a serious one; if detrimental effects can be foreseen (as where there is a history of many losses) some alternative to college counseling may be early decided on: an early referral or postponement of therapy. In other cases discussion of the anticipated reaction to termination may prepare the student to handle it when it comes. Some students will "forget" that a time limit exists, in spite of repeated reminders; others will plead for continuation as private patients with the parents' joining in the plea. For some the existence of the time limit is from the start a proof of the counselor's unconcern and an argument against getting personally involved in counseling. Others will make the issue of termination a focus of an open struggle with the counselor, aimed at achieving an exceptional position or at enforcing one's will. Instead of the counselor the administration may be viewed as the enforcer of the rule, the student proposing to start a movement to effect a general extension of counseling periods. Some students will become acutely upset after termination and refuse to accept help from any but their former counselor. In most of these cases the counselor who remains uninvolved in the struggle has a good opportunity to clarify to himself and to the student the nature and implications of the patterns being acted out. For some students the working through of the conflicts and struggles developing around the issue of termination and referral has at least as much therapeutic effect as the work done previously, or in the interval between such episodes.

For a certain proportion of students counseling is terminated by a *forced or voluntary withdrawal from school,* usually in connection with academic failure, or near failure. Many of these students anticipate this outcome and enter counseling in an attempt to avert it, thus presenting the counselor with another kind of deadline. The student's initial centering on one practical goal makes for a slow start, and the frequently present lifelong pattern of under-achievement rarely permits quick success. Often one must be satisfied with the student's having obtained sufficient insight into the cause of his failure to make some realistic — even if not final — decision: to modify his educational plans, to try and work out his problems in therapy before re-entering college. Some students persistently deny the degree of their handicap, bolstering themselves with the knowledge of their high intelligence scores, for instance, and attributing their poor grades to a variety of external circumstances; for them the shock of severance if well worked out in terminal sessions may lead to productive results.

Some students decide to leave school before catastrophe overtakes them, or for reasons other than a realistic threat of failure. In the latter case, particularly with academically successful students, some pressure against such decision is often exercised by the school. The counselor must take care to divorce himself from these influences and remain open to the student's feelings. His decision to withdraw is often the result of a long struggle with internal conflicts and may be the best solution possible for him at the time.

A son of a successful father preoccupied with business and community affairs continually missed classes and read only books that were not assigned in courses; he was heading towards failure and this course was clearly directed against his father. Attempts at clarifying his motives did not lead to improvement, but eventually led to a decision to withdraw voluntarily in order to forestall failure, and to enter outside therapy. A few months later the student wrote the counselor of a dramatic discovery: he wanted to anger his father in order to test his love and to get some evidence of his interest, even if it were anger. A year later he entered another college.

While not opposing the student's decision, the counselor must insist within reason that it should be talked through, some realistic plans formulated, and the student's chances for re-entering college protected. In the rare event of a student withdrawing abruptly both from counseling and from school the counselor's intervention may mitigate the self-destructive aspect of the step and the resulting sense of failure.

A student felt inadequate and unworthy of being financed by a large fellowship, despite the achievement of a brilliant academic record. She experienced severe depressions and only with extensive therapeutic support was she able to remain in school. During Christmas vacation she became so fearful and blocked that she decided to remain at home and not return to take her forthcoming examinations.

Withdrawal at this time might have ended her college career on a note of failure. A series of letters and telephone calls from the counselor persuaded her to return to campus and to take some of the examinations. She passed them and was given a leave of absence from school, with permission to return when she felt ready. A year later she re-entered school.

The task of *referring students to outside therapists* after a period of college counseling presents difficulties which are the obverse of the influences facilitating the entrance into counseling. What is involved is not only changing the therapist: the whole implication of the therapeutic endeavor may change for the student when it is transplanted from the familiar school setting to an outside agency. Sacrifices demanded in terms of time and money and the necessity to involve parents underline the importance of the undertaking; the student may feel that if such sacrifices are warranted he must be seriously ill. Separation of therapy from the semi-familial school environment may frighten and repel a dependent student who feels that he is being pushed out into an unknown cold world. When such negative implications are strong in the student's mind the process of arriving at the decision to continue therapy may be accompanied by significant experiences and insights. Students whose whole period of counseling work was in the nature of pre-counseling may on this occasion acknowledge for the first time their serious need for help. Dependence on the family may be brought a step closer to resolution. As in other stages parents may actively involve themselves in the issue of transfer.

A student hesitantly decided to go into therapy. When a therapist was found whom he immediately liked, his mother became worried; she called the counselor to complain of her son being sent to a stranger. After that the student became upset and tried to coax the counselor to see him for six more sessions, promising to transfer at the end of this period. He was afraid to give up the security and comfort of the familiar

Specific Features of Therapeutic Work

relationship, just as he had been afraid to be away from home and mother. When the student was able to see the relationship between his past and present behavior, he begrudgingly decided to transfer to the new therapist.

To be handled successfully, the issue of referral, like that of termination, must be worked on in advance. In most cases it can be introduced, as an impersonal possibility, when the conditions of counseling are first discussed, and later brought up, repeatedly if necessary, in relation to the student himself. Timing of the suggestion is of the essence. It has little chance even to be considered by the student, unless and until he has experienced some progress in counseling. On the other hand, if continuation is strongly indicated, the issue must be brought up early enough to permit the student to work out his misgivings about therapy before the end of the year. The problem should be explored like any other issue that comes up in counseling. Too much discussion or pushing of the plan by the counselor may lead to futile struggles, or to a spurious acceptance by the student. He may agree, but postpone action, or indecisively shop around for therapists, rejecting each one in turn. If the issue has not been resolved by the end of the year, the student may be invited to return for a few sessions in the fall, for help in arriving at some decision. With some clinging students we found it profitable to have them discuss these plans with a different counselor, or with the college psychiatrist, in order to emphasize that this discussion is not meant as an extension of counseling. Some students act on the idea at a much later date, approaching the counselor for help in referral some years after having left college.

In cases of immediate referral the students usually appreciate the opportunity to see the counselor once or twice after having made contact with the new therapist. The overlap makes the transition more comfortable and helps to resolve the individual problems involved in termination and transfer. Some of the feelings about the new therapist can be worked out with the counselor and acceptance of the new relationship facilitated. At a later time, during episodes of negative transference, some students have discontinued with their therapist and returned to the counselor. In most of these cases a few sessions are enough for them to work through their resistance and to return into therapy, although in some exceptional cases the counselor may be called upon to act as a mediator between the student and his therapist.

IV

THE RELATION OF PSYCHOLOGY COURSES TO COUNSELING

Richard M. Jones

It was noted above that a dynamically oriented and popular Psychology Department brings certain general influences to bear on the work of the Counseling Center. Vaguely defined aspirations towards self-improvement, which are frequently prominent in the decisions of students to enroll in psychology courses, may become more articulate. Autobiographical and introspective assignments may crystallize personal problems. General information about processes of personality development may further define covert hopes and fears in this area, and prospects of professionally guided self-discovery may come to be relieved of accumulated stigmatic associations. Finally, students who are enrolled in psychology courses which are taught by members of the counseling staff may more comfortably explore the feasibility of counseling via consultation with a teacher. On the negative side, the psychology courses provide a vocabulary with which some students may go through many fruitless motions of "self-analysis," the undoing of which may then be the task of pre-counseling efforts. All of these general influences are brought more directly to bear on the work of the Center by virtue of its formal status as an adjunct of the Psychology Department.

We turn now to a detailed discussion of the *specific* implications for the work of counseling of *certain* psychology courses in which modified group psychotherapeutic discussion techniques are employed as pedagogic devices. In three courses (Child

Psychology, Educational Psychology, and Theories of Personality) students may elect to participate in weekly free discussion meetings in addition to the usual section meetings based on lectures and readings. The rationale for these free discussion meetings centers around the problem of assimilative learning, and has been summarized as follows:

To assimilate a subject is to make that subject one's own; to cognize it in one's own manner, such that one may re-cognize it in the various "realistic" forms in which nature and society may present it. It is this knack for pushing other people's conclusions around before "grasping" them for oneself that the teacher, often not a stranger to it himself, is typically unable to instill in his students — unable, sometimes, less for want of ambition in this regard than for want of methods designed to achieve that ambition. The problem of assimilative learning is particularly urgent for the teacher of psychology, by virtue of the lurking questions that partially motivate his classes. Questions like: "What's wrong with me?" "What can I do about it?" "What's right with me?" "What can I do with it?" etc. To turn such self-seeking questions to the advantage of assimilating "psychology" is to embark on a course in which education and psychotherapy become overlapping, albeit separately definable, processes. I refer to such modifications of traditional pedagogy as the construction of examinations which involve analogical as well as logical study habits, and of assignments which engage preconscious processes (dreams, fantasies, images, etc.) as well as their conscious derivatives. I refer also to the application of group psychotherapeutic methods to classroom discussions; for example: contracted responsibility to pursue relevant self-knowledge; periodic emphasis on total freedom of expression; and a corresponding emphasis on articulating the conflicts thus inevitably aroused.

Ernest Jones, in his paper "The Genesis of Superego," describes a prototypic situation which is germane to this approach.[1] It is the situation of the young infant, confronted on the one hand by vast though limited external powers (his parents), and on the other hand by vast and unlimited internal powers (his fantasies). The infant introjects the parental images as basic guides to experience, but not until he has invested those images with the powers of his own imagination. As Jones put it: "The introjections are what constitute the superego, but — and this is a most essential point — they are far from simple incorporations of external realities, but are to a greater extent incorporations of the infant's projections as well." In other words, we pre-form in our own manner those very symbols of parental authority which we then borrow as a foundation for self-discipline. Seen in this light prototypic superego formation is the foundation both of ego defense and of assimilative learning. It is insofar as psychotherapy seeks to re-organize the former and education to organize the latter that the two technologies are separately definable. It is insofar as both must deal with a common psychogenetic root that they overlap.

The same conclusion emerges from a second point of view: Jones' reformulation of superego formation generates a definition of anxiety as the condition of being alone and helpless in the presence of imagination. The parameters of aloneness and helplessness, and the qualities of imagination, of course, change with age. The infant's aloneness may only be assuaged at times by the touch of skin on skin; his helplessness in the presence of his own fantasies by the inclusion among them of fantastically inflated parental injunctions. Later on, aloneness may give way to the representations of others, i.e., to knowledge; and helplessness to an enlightened conscience, i.e., to insight. It bears

---

[1] Jones, Ernest. "The Genesis of the Superego," in Thompson, Mayer, and Wittenberg (eds.), *An Outline of Psychoanalysis*. New York: The Modern Library, 1955.

emphasis, however, that anxiety at any age is the condition of being *both* alone and helpless, *and* in the presence of *imagination*. Against this theoretical backdrop, group psychotherapy and education may be considered complementary aspects of any interaction between a group and its leader when the intent of the leader is not to exploit the superego, which ultimately, however unrealistically, establishes his authority, but to redeem its derivative patterns of submissiveness, self-belittlement, and intellectual timidity, in favor of more mature patterns of mutuality. The therapeutic aspects of this interaction, as they transform misconceptions of fantasy into insight, make for an ability to feel less helpless when necessarily alone. The educational aspects, as they replace glorification of authority with exemplary models, special competencies, command of scientific and ethical principles, etc., make for an ability to feel less alone when necessarily helpless.

To this end, the author has sought to construct a classroom situation in which patterns of resistance and transference are mobilized in such ways as to be conducive in their resolution to heightened assimilation of the subject matter. These classes (hereafter referred to as laboratory groups) are led by the author, who is both an experienced group therapist and a member of the counseling staff, and by supervised graduate students.

Student membership in laboratory groups is optional. The following excerpts from one student's notes will communicate something of the flavor of the meetings:

> Bill was called on to read his minutes from last time. However, he didn't have any, and instead explained the relevance of a book he had read to the group sessions (Flugel's *Psychoanalytic Study of the Family*). The book states that in any group there is a recipient of the emotional energy within the group. In a family the recipient or target is usually the father; in the classroom, the teacher. Here it has been Nancy.

Nancy then called our attention to the fact that she had *previously* brought up the same idea of this group as compared to a family constellation. Dr. J. said it takes a while for some ideas to take root.

Nancy then brought up the child's painting that we had seen in the section meeting. Dr. J. had pointed out that a teacher would not be well-advised to tell a child that his picture revealed such and such; we can see what happens when this is done by looking at what has transpired in the lab. Telling someone what they mean before they understand it themselves isn't any good. (For example, as Nancy said, my paper "taking her apart and putting her together again" and Mike telling her how she is.) You can't just throw something at someone like that. It seems to be the job of the teacher not to explain but rather to give the student tools with which to understand.

Mike led the discussion back to the idea of each group having one or more members as recipients of its emotional energy. He asked Bill if the clown of the group is also such a recipient, for he had been the clown in several meetings. Bill said he didn't think so. Nancy, referring to Erikson's theory, said that clowns remind us of our past falls; we laugh at them instead of at ourselves.

Bill then noted that in our group both Nancy and Mike have received our hostility, that his past questions to Mike weren't just curiosity. Nancy agreed; neither had hers been. I said that I had asked Mike questions because his opinions were different from mine — that it had been sort of an airing out of opinions.

At this point, Nancy brought up the notion of transference and its relevance here. She explained that when we attack someone with our emotions irrationally, without knowing why at the time, and when all our feelings are concentrated on this one person, it is often a transference phenomenon. She then gave as an example her previous attacks on Dr. J.; she had *had* to attack him but for no rational reason — she had not understood why at the time; all she had known was that she had to. Teachers are often such emotional targets for their students. She then gave another example — in elementary school she attacked her teachers a great deal; she lived in a very rigid, disciplined home in which she was not allowed to express herself and she took it out the only place she could — on her teachers. Later, she lived in a much better atmosphere and her attacks on the teachers ceased.

Mike then mentioned that he hadn't realized that anyone had had any pins out, so to speak; that he hadn't felt any attacks directed toward him. Sally affirmed that there had been some; that Mike got asked more questions than others. Mike said he thought that it was luck that brought more questions. Bill noted that Mike's opinions had deviated from the norm — and that the deviant always gets attacked. Mary noted that Mike also was freer in asking questions and admitting things he didn't understand, which the rest of us are more inhibited in doing. As we grow up we are "pushed down" from asking questions. She admires him for asking; it shows he is still interested. I agree.

Mary then asked what was going on in the last meeting (she had been absent for the past two meetings). Mike tried to explain what had occurred. She then mentioned that everyone had made a point of saying something to her about missing the meeting. She couldn't understand why everyone had gone out of their way to ask why she wasn't present. Bill said he thought she was "chickening" out. Dr. J. asked Mary what she felt in the questions. She answered: "Venom." Bill then noted that she had deviated from the norm with her absence, so again we were back to Flugel's theory of a recipient of group energy.

In some instances these laboratory groups serve in a recruitment capacity for the Center. This is usually unproblematic. Insofar as an atmosphere of comparative intimacy and self-confrontation prevails in the group meetings the students are afforded an opportunity to sample something akin to the atmosphere of counseling. If subsequently a student who has been a member of one of these groups inquires about counseling he can be referred to his own experience, being informed, for example, that the confidentiality of counseling sessions permits greater personal commitment and focus than the group session, but that the two have certain similarities. The mystique of psychological counseling is thus tangibly dispelled for some students in a context associated with normal academic pursuits.

There are occasional instances when the engendering of a semi-therapeutic atmosphere in the classroom confronts a student with personal issues before he is ready to commit himself to the effort of their conscious resolution. A particularly sensitive problem of referral to the Center is then posed.

For example, during an early group session in Child Psychology in which the students were discussing the motives that might have led them to choose a particular Nursery School child to observe, one boy straight-facedly stated that he may have chosen the lone wolf because he himself never had anyone to play with as a boy, even though he was one of three brothers. At this, as though suddenly realizing some privately disturbing implication, he became visibly upset, and, despite the group's efforts to rally to his support (which is typical of these groups in such a situation), he remained sufficiently disturbed to spend the instructor's next office hour revealing a very trying home situation. One of his brothers was mentally defective; the other hospitalized with a diagnosis of schizophrenia. The exclusive point of these disclosures was his concern for his brothers. The instructor hinted that *anyone* in such a troubled family might feel some pressures of his own. To this there was no response. Nevertheless the instructor described the Counseling Center to him and made an offer to arrange an appointment should he ever wish it. One year later the offer was taken up, and the boy's senior year included a useful period of personal counseling.

Two points bear emphasis here: (1) When a student approaches the Center as the result of some conflict or crisis in the laboratory sessions, the instructor should be especially careful not to press the student to begin personal counseling, as the precipitating motives may not clearly be felt by the student to be personally relevant. (2) Having utilized such meetings with individual students to make the Center's services known to the student, the instructor should make himself readily available as an intermediary between that student and the Center in the future.

The laboratory groups have sometimes served to facilitate the referral of students whose previous experience at the Center had been insufficiently helpful:

A boy who was expert in alienating his peers entered counseling in his junior year. His approach to the counselor was one of watching the counselor's "techniques." Forthwith, he began to apply these techniques with troubled boys in his dormitory. Becoming, so he felt, an overnight success as the self-appointed dormitory psychiatrist, he prematurely terminated his own counseling sessions. The following semester he enrolled in a laboratory group in the Theories of Personality course. Immediately he set about making enemies of his colleagues by adopting the role of non-participant observer and inquisitor-at-large. As an atmosphere of cohesiveness developed in the group, the sighs, whispers, and dirty looks gave way to explicit expressions of irritation by the other group members: he was "a burden to the group," a "Peeping-Tom type," who "would be better advised to gain some insight into yourself before going around examining others." In retreat before these charges, and by way of refuting them, the boy disclosed that so far from considering himself above the aims of the group, he had even been to the Counseling Center and had in fact learned a lot about himself. He then volunteered, much to the amazed relief of the others, that the reason he had sought help in the first place was his inability to make friends! At that moment the boy's position in the group changed from outside irritant to inside irritant; and although this disclosure was not again raised in the group the instructor had several subsequent occasions to meet the boy coming away from his resumed counseling sessions.

It is characteristic of the laboratory groups that the distinction between free discussion as a means toward deepened comprehension of the course materials and as an inappropriate end in itself tends to become blurred. Sometimes this takes the form of a conscious and expressed resolve on the part of some students to turn the meeting into group therapy sessions: "We can always get section meetings but it isn't every class that we can use to learn about ourselves." Sometimes the pressures are less explicit, becoming manifest, for example, in provocative self-revelations or the acting out of personal involvements which are refractory on their face to utilization as illustrations in point of the subject matter. It is, of course, one of the instructor's primary responsibilities in these groups to keep in focus the discrepancies between such pressures and the agreed-upon and binding academic purpose of the meetings. Indeed it is precisely the highlighted emergence of such discrepancies, and their ultimate correction, that constitute the special pedagogical leverage of these groups; thus their designation as "laboratory" groups. In the process, however, areas of overlap between the work of the Counseling Center and the work of the psychology classes have been observed, which are problematic for both.

Students concurrently in counseling may be tempted to utilize their group membership as supplementary to their counseling sessions. This can work to the advantage of all concerned.

> For example, a very mature girl who was much respected by her classmates was working intensively and well in counseling on certain emotional crises involved in simultaneously achieving independence from an overly solicitous family, feeling her way in her first deeply felt love relationship, and containing anxiety over an approaching serious operation. She found the Child Psychology laboratory meetings to be especially helpful in providing substantive material for her counseling sessions, and also as a ready testing ground for new insights. The counselor concurred that this was so. The group was unaware that she was in counseling until one session midway in the semester when several members were pressing for a group decision to discount academic purposes in order to explore more personal issues. It was this girl's informed opinion, as she put it, that such a decision would be a mistake. It was an informed opinion, she continued, because she was also in counseling and found the group meeting under the present arrangement very helpful. But she did not think the group meetings would be very effective *without* individual counseling, and besides, she took the course primarily to learn something about child development, and would feel cheated if this were not to remain the primary aim of the group. The group's response was unified: "You, the healthiest girl on campus, go to the Counseling Center?"

Three purposes were thus served: (1) The group meetings did enhance this girl's counseling work, (2) the group was re-

The Relation of Psychology Courses to Counseling

oriented to its own responsibilities more effectively than could have been engineered by the instructor, (3) the image of the Center as a service utilized by normal students was dramatically reinforced.

In another case the group meetings were helpful in the therapy of one student, but at the expense of the group.

> A girl was referred by the Center to a private psychoanalyst when a diagnosis of latent *anorexia nervosa* was suspected. Two years later, still in analysis, she enrolled in a laboratory group of the Theories of Personality course. It became clear in the first session that the depth and force of this girl's unwitting emotional demands might be out of line with the group's educative design. (For example: "I've spent 19 years feeling it was wrong to be close to anyone, and now that I realize it isn't, I find that I don't know how to reverse old habits. Signing up for this group is the first time I've openly admitted that I want people to know me.") The instructor planned to ask the girl to postpone taking the course for a year but consulted first with the girl's analyst. It was the analyst's opinion that if the group could possibly contain the girl her treatment would greatly benefit as a consequence. Losing sight with the analyst of the very distinction that he was normally at pains to maintain with the students, the instructor agreed to try it. It developed that *only* a therapeutic group could have contained this girl, which it did, much to the unenlightening confusion of the other group members. So sensitive and so unerringly accurate was she in perceiving the normally defensive postures taken by the other group members in respect to feelings of intimacy, but also so unrestrained was she in exposing these postures that the instructor had frequently to take steps which were singularly designed for the support and control of this one member. It was not surprising, therefore to hear from another member

at the end of the course: "At the same time that I was going to counseling I was taking a psych. lab. course (108a) that I felt to be pure Hell every minute of every session. Counseling, in a sense, had to overcome *this* as well as the usual me. It has taken nearly a full year to undo the effects of this learning experience. But perhaps it may have helped bring to the surface many areas of anxiety that I might not have probed myself."

Another case illustrates how the two activities can interact to mutual advantage, provided the instructor and the counselor involved consult with each other — an arrangement that is only possible, of course, if the instructor is on the counseling staff.

An older student entered counseling at a time when he was on the point of failing out of school for the third time. It developed that a suppressed set of anti-intellectual attitudes was associated with repressed and heavily defended dependency wishes — all of this finding symptomatic expression in excessive drinking and an emotional block against the reading of scholarly books. It happened that he began to show signs in counseling of beginning to work on the underlying components of the problem at the time when he enrolled in a laboratory group of the Educational Psychology course. The counselor alerted the instructor to the situation and mentioned in passing that he was bewildered by the man's complacency in the counseling sessions. He would appreciate, he said, any tips based on outside observations as to how he might elicit the man's more active involvement in therapy. It was soon clear to the instructor why it was that this student's anti-dependent and anti-intellectual attitudes were missing from his counseling sessions: they were finding easier expression in the group. For example: "You people who want to sit around here and talk about yourselves are just a bunch of babies. If you want help with your personal problems, go to the Counseling Center, don't look for it here. And don't give me any stuff from that nut Kubie either. That book of his is the worst garbage I ever paid good money for." Had the instructor not been briefed about this student's current behavior in counseling he might have reacted differently. As it was, however, these outbursts were clearly identifiable as displacements from therapy. Knowing therefore that the man could safely — even strategically — be exposed to the sobering medicine that only peers can administer, the instructor proceeded to favor him in slight ways that were calculated to bring the wrath of scapegoatism down upon him — referring to him, for example, as the group's "emotional barometer" and asking from time to time for "a reading." The machinations of group dynamics were not long in taking the cue. The next time he belittled the members who were appropriately pressing for greater candor in the group, he was treated to the following, complete with finger-wagging, from a very outspoken young lady sitting across from him: "Listen, you barometer or whatever you're supposed to be, you are the last person here that should be calling anybody a baby. You make a lot of noise, but every time you open your mouth you're asking everyone here to feed it. So from now on, when feeding time comes you just wait your goddam turn." For all its acidity this was not without affection, and the man's position in the group was sufficiently strong to stand up to it. The effects, however, were two fold: (1) the candor of the group meetings did increase, (2) the counselor was soon reporting the kind of stormy sessions he had hoped for in this case.

The association of the Counseling Center with these classes by way of both substantive and misinterpreted similarities carries two disadvantages. A student who is militantly unsympathetic to counseling as a means of working out personal problems, may elect to enroll in a group, whereupon he proceeds to prove the soundness of his initial attitude to himself and to anyone else who can be convinced. A situation of violated trust, for example, may be provoked within the group, and then used as evidence that counseling is not truly confidential. As clinical confidentiality is not a part of the laboratory agreements, the charge is irrelevant and can even be worked to educational advantage in the group. However, were the instructor to defend the Counseling Center before the group against such guilt by association it would probably serve only to support the association in the eyes of the other students. The instructor must therefore be content to clarify the misinterpretation in terms of the group's purposes, leaving the spurious involvement of the Center to shift for itself. This does not pose a singular problem as regards the student body at large, as rumors of this kind are inevitable and are only effectively dealt with by seeing to it that they are unfounded. However, were it not that the laboratory meetings can lend themselves to this misuse, some students might attempt to confirm their fears at the source, where they would stand a better chance of being dispelled. Conversely, there are students who view counseling very sympathetically, and who might otherwise profitably use the service themselves, were it not that the laboratory sections may be misinterpreted as offering a kind of therapy. One boy, for example, convinced several of his friends to enter counseling on the basis of his group experience. He himself was content to see the soundness of his advice confirmed by their good reports. He finally made an appointment for counseling with his former instructor six weeks before his graduation. A successful referral was made, but he and the instructor both had reason to be irritated with the opportunity that was lost largely as a result of his successful experience in the group.

Finally, there is the amusing case of the sophomore who was

so impressed with her group experience that she wanted desperately to begin counseling as a way of continuing what the group had started. However, she complained, she didn't think it would work if she began counseling on a false note, and the truth of the matter was she had no problems. Resisting the temptation to count the absence of problems as a problem sufficient in itself, the counselor advised that she give herself until her junior year to develop a problem and then come in again. At this writing she is scheduled for her first appointment.

In conclusion, if it appears from the above that we have undertaken a roundabout way of combining group and individual therapy, let us hasten to emphasize that we have focussed here exclusively on those aspects of the laboratory groups which indirectly interact with the work of the Counseling Center.[2] The primary effectiveness of the laboratory groups as pedagogical tools for mobilizing personal motives in the service of academic study in the behavioral sciences has been reported in detail elsewhere.[3]

[2] A study of coordinated individual and group counseling in the college setting, now in exploratory stages, is being conducted by Dr. David Ricks with the support of funds donated for this purpose by Mr. William Heller.

[3] See Jones, R. M. *An Application of Psychoanalysis to Education,* Springfield, Ill.: Thomas Publishing Co., 1960; "The Role of Self-knowledge in the Educative Process", *Harvard Educational Review,* Vol. 32, No. 2, 1962; and "Some Educational Aspects of Group-Leader Interaction", Eastern Group Psychotherapy Assn., in press.

V

CONCLUDING REMARKS

Our experience has shown that if certain conditions are fulfilled the setting of a small residential college permits an extension of mental health work to students who may be expected to benefit from it maximally: those whose difficulties, though not extreme, prevent their continued growth into adulthood and presage neurotic limitations and distortions in the future. Their proportion in the student population is more difficult to estimate than that of the extremely disturbed. We can, however, make some estimates of the extent to which the counseling program at Brandeis has succeeded in reaching this group of students for whose development early help might be crucial.

Of the class graduating in 1962, 25% had received some help from the Counseling Center in the course of their college career; if one includes those who left school before graduation this proportion is raised to $c.$ 30% of the class of '62 at its maximum size. Roughly one-sixth of these students (or 5% of the class) showed a degree of disturbance that might sooner or later bring them to psychiatric attention. This group includes both those whose personality disturbance was chronic and was rated by us as severe and those who were acutely but only briefly disturbed at the time when they applied for help. The remaining group, a rather bright and academically successful group of students, would certainly qualify as free from any psychiatric disturbance. Within this group about one-fourth of the students (or 6% of the class) were rated as having a "slight disturbance," which in many cases meant no noticeable emotional disturbance at all. The help which these students required for meeting some circumscribed problem, situational or developmental, was limited in scope and consisted essentially in an opportunity to discuss the issue with an understanding and informed adult; such help could have been given by a person who had no specialized training and skills. Doubtless this kind of help is being given students by some of their teachers, particularly in school settings that permit frequent informal contacts between the faculty and the students.

When the most and the least disturbed are accounted for there remains the large middle group of students whose disturbance was rated as "moderate"; it contains about 65% of the students seen or about 20% of the class. In this group we find both pronounced cases of adolescent struggles and crises and neurotic personality patterns that are neither extreme nor incapacitating. This is the group which maximally utilizes the opportunity for prolonged counseling and which probably benefits from it most. Cases in which therapeutic progress is very obvious to the student and to the counselor very often come from this group. Some of these students had thought about the possibility of therapy in the future, but for the majority of this group it can be stated with certainty that in the absence of an opportunity provided by the school they would not have sought professional help for their difficulties at this period of their lives, and probably not until much later, if indeed at all.

One may assume that some of these young people will outgrow their difficulties in time with the help of "therapeutic factors" which life itself may offer. Still, the wide prevalence of emotional disturbances in the "normal" adult population puts limits on the optimistic outlook which a college mental health worker tends to develop when confronted with the developmental vigor of this age group. There is good evidence that this vigor soon abates and that no significant personality changes can be expected to take place in the majority after the college years are over. In this context one finding of the study of

Vassar alumnae 20 to 25 years after graduation is of particular interest. It was found that those women who during their college years fitted our present conception of "identity seekers" — a group which in therapy often makes vigorous strides — "have been unable to arrive at stable lives except after prolonged therapy or drastic change in the environment, or both. The families were either unstable or oppressive, or the sex-role conflict was so severe and sex identities so muddled that normal heterosexual relations were seriously impaired. These are the subjects who as students presumably could have profited most from currently existing therapeutic facilities on the campus."[1] We cannot hope to bring objective proof of the long term efficacy of our work with a similar group of students: this would require not only elaborate follow-up studies, but also a research design of matched student groups of which only one would receive counseling help, a design that is not feasible in a service setting. Yet all available evidence makes it seem likely that students who had a successful period of short therapy in college have saved themselves much fruitless trouble in later life or a much longer period of therapeutic work in later adulthood.

What are the conditions that must be fulfilled in the setting of a small college if skilled counseling help is to reach the large group of students who are likely to benefit from it most? Apart from the obvious condition of providing ample time for all comers — which can only be met if the services of trained nonmedical therapists are utilized on a large scale — all these conditions pertain to factors that lead to the acceptance of psychological counseling and to its integration with the existing peer culture of the students. Any measure that tends to remove the stigma of abnormality from the participants in counseling, e.g., by identifying it as an educational rather than as a corrective

---

[1] Brown, Donald R. "Personality, College Environment, and Academic Productivity," in Nevitt, Sanford (ed.), *The American College.* New York: John Wiley & Sons, Inc., 1962.

process, can be of help in achieving this goal. The crucial condition, however, is a clear-cut separation of counseling from all administrative concerns. In the compact community of a small campus school where news travels fast, the implementation of this general principle and of all other policies involving the students must be particularly stringent and clear. It is not enough for the counselor to assure the student of the confidentiality of the sessions and to promise to use his discretion in any discussion of his case with the administration: this may be sufficient for many, particularly if their need is urgent. The students as a whole, however, will not accept the service as theirs to use if the counselors are known to have an active consultative relationship with the administration which includes a discussion of individual cases. A service that aims at reaching large numbers of students must accept this situation as a fact.

If this is genuinely accepted by the administration as well, the limitation creates few real problems. Situations that clearly require consultation with other school offices are rare, particularly if time is available for the student to work on his problem in counseling until he is ready to be his own spokesman. In other cases the need to involve the administration, or the parents, can be determined by the student and the counselor together and carried out as a common project. As long as nothing is done behind the student's back, without his genuine consent, these occasional exceptions do not violate the intent of the general policy and will not cause misunderstanding. On the other hand, any hope that the mental health worker may have of effectively combining the therapeutic with an administratively tinged role in a small traditionally run school is unrealistic. The counselor himself may be able to keep distinct his treatment of those students who come to him on their own and to whom he owes full confidentiality, from his procedures with those who are referred by the administration with a view to consultation. He cannot, however, expect the students to maintain this double image without confusion, and confusion about the counselor's role is the surest deterrent to the students' utilization of that role. A clear public explanation of the differential policy might counteract confusion, and the distribution of the two roles between different persons or different units of the mental health service might be expected to be of help. However, the effectiveness of such measures is very limited; this is not astonishing if one considers that at the times when the administration is seen by the student as an enemy the two roles in question are not just different but emotionally incompatible: "if he is for them he is against us." While the first College Psychiatrist at Brandeis experimented with the possibilities of fulfilling the administration's wish for consultation on individual students, the policies of the Psychological Counseling Center which clearly exclude such consultation remained unaltered. Nevertheless, the confusion and suspicion engendered in the minds of the students during this period spread also to the work of the Center. Both mental health services were accused by some of being administration stooges or sources of illegal power in the school. On the other hand, those students who had built up confidence in the Center were the more inclined to make the Psychiatrist the real villain of the play; the image of one of the services suffered either by being merged or by being contrasted with the other. Whether or not the problem of consulting with the administration can be solved by segregating this function from the therapeutic service, it is abundantly clear that for a counseling center which works with the relatively healthy, well functioning student, any advantages of working with and through the administration are not worth the price that must be paid in student trust.

If the conditions of this trust are met and steadily maintained a growing utilization of counseling services by the students can be confidently expected. Some factors, internal and external, put limits on this growth. We know from the students that some of the very disturbed ones do not come; certain groups reject counseling for ideological reasons; the limited duration of college counseling is a strong objection of a few, and the impossibility of complete privacy is an irksome point and perhaps a deterrent for many. These drawbacks are lamented and criticized by the students, but they are not insurmountable obstacles to an eventual acceptance of psychological counseling as a natural part of the college scene. The following description by a student reflects changes in the perception of the Center that took place during her years in college.

> When the Center was in Ridgewood there seemed to be an air of mystery surrounding it. This is possibly because at that time I didn't know anyone who was going. At first I had assumed that you really had to have a big psychic disorder to go and I think I even attached some sort of stigma to the whole idea. During the last few years I have heard not terribly much more about the Center, but the conversation seems to have changed in character; the Center seems to be accepted as a useful service — even at times "the 'cool' thing to do." I was surprised at the number of my friends who had been there at least once. . . .

After a certain degree of acceptance has been achieved by the service the students themselves become the most active source of referrals. Barring any unsettling developments the attendance tends to grow. During the last school year the joint mental health services at Brandeis were used by 18% of all undergraduates, which is more than double that of ten years ago, and the percent was roughly the same for each of the four classes. If this rate of participation should remain stable, and assuming an overlap of one third between the groups counseled in contiguous years, approximately one half of the class to graduate four years hence will have made use of the mental health services. With this rate of participation we can feel confident of reaching a large proportion of those students to whom early help can be maximally beneficial.

Wide student participation in counseling results in some problems of its own on a small campus when friends or acquaintances enter counseling simultaneously and may find themselves seeing the same counselor. The counseling staff must keep alert to the interrelationships and interactions of the counselees in order to avoid or minimize this unplanned-for "group aspect" of counseling or to handle involvements resulting from it. Yet the participation of friends has proven of great value both in a range of ordinary situations and in emergencies; some acutely disturbed students, including those harboring suicidal thoughts, reach the Center through the often very active and ingenious efforts of friends.

College mental health workers are often asked how the incidence and kind of student disturbances which they see compare with those observed in other schools. Apart from the paucity of published data, this question could only be answered if the school services were roughly equal at least with regard to the amount of available time per student, and with regard to the general policies in relation to the administration. The use of different classifications by different schools also makes comparisons difficult. The channels and methods of referral which may be a function of policy factors in turn determine the selection of students who will be seen by the service. This is illustrated by one clear-cut difference between the students presenting complaints at Brandeis and at Harvard. More than half of the students seen by the psychiatrists of the Health Service at Harvard complain primarily of difficulties in studying, or of emotional reactions clearly related to them;[2] at Brandeis the

---

[2] Blaine, G. B., and McArthur, C. C. "Problems Connected with Studying," Blaine and McArthur (eds.), in *Emotional Problems of the Student,* New York: Appleton-Century-Crofts, 1961, Ch. 5, p. 76.

incidence of complaints centered on academic difficulties is much lower, averaging around 15% and never exceeding 25%. One is easily tempted to attribute this difference to differential academic pressures, or academic ambitions, or other factors inherent in the character of the schools and of the populations they select and form. We note, however, that among men at Brandeis complaints about studies are more frequent than is indicated by averages which include women. They are also more frequent among those who are referred by the Student Personnel or by the faculty than among those who come on their own; we assume that the same relationship holds at Harvard. Since the proportion of undergraduates referred through school channels is 66% at Harvard and 20% at Brandeis the different incidence of complaints about studies may be explained by the combination of the sex factor and the school referral factor. Similarly the participation of girls may account for the predominance at Brandeis of concerns about difficulties in personal relations and, among those with neurotic patterns, for the predominance of hysterical pictures over the compulsive. Finally the observation that, as compared with Harvard, an even smaller proportion of the students seen at Brandeis could be fitted into some psychiatric category, is consistent with the fact that we are able to see a much larger proportion of the undergraduate student body and try to encourage participation of those whose needs are not urgently pressing. Taking all these differences into account we are impressed by the inferrable similarities in the incidence and nature of emotional disturbances encountered in the two schools. A more detailed comparative analysis would no doubt uncover important differences as well.

In conclusion a word about the main sources of satisfaction and frustration of a mental health worker in a small college. He may have to go through a hard struggle to establish and to maintain conditions that are essential for the success of his work; in this process he will sometimes have to bear the brunt both of the students' and the administration's anxieties. He himself may be frustrated by the limitations which the situation of a small school imposes on the work he might like to do with the administrative officers or faculty members, although these very limitations might induce him to work out better methods for stimulating psychological understanding in those who concern themselves with the students. He does not lose much of value by having to withhold advice or by renouncing conventional teaching. But whatever frustrations he feels they will be more than balanced by the chance to devote his time to direct therapeutic work with a group of most promising clients. More often than a therapist working in any other setting, he will be a participant observer of either steadily unfolding or dramatically sudden progress; he will have a greater measure of freedom than would be his in working with the more seriously ill to depart from the methods he has learned and to take his cues from his client and himself. In some cases an informal follow-up will give him the satisfaction of knowing that the work done had been sufficient to insure the student's continued personal growth. For others the period of counseling will be too brief to bring about the desired results. These cases present the counselor with the challenge of making this first experience of therapy sufficiently vital and rewarding to pave the way to its continuation or later resumption. This challenge, together with the existence of the time limit, counteracts the tendency to relax into careless ways which the counselor may develop in working with people who move so readily by themselves; it puts pressure on him to use both his skills and his opportunities to the best advantage in an attempt to make counseling personally meaningful to every student with whom he works.

APPENDIX

SOME QUESTIONS AND ANSWERS ABOUT PSYCHOLOGICAL COUNSELING AND ABOUT THE PSYCHOLOGICAL COUNSELING CENTER OF BRANDEIS UNIVERSITY

WHAT IS THE MAIN AIM OF COUNSELING?

Counseling aims at bringing about greater self-awareness for the solution of personal or emotional problems.

IS IT A SIGN OF BEING ABNORMAL TO NEED COUNSELING?

The fear that one might be abnormal, or that others would think so, is quite common. Most of the people who come to the Center* are not in danger of becoming mentally ill and can't be considered abnormal by any criteria. They may be merely more aware of having unsolved problems than many others who have very similar difficulties, but don't realize that matters could be improved.

WHAT KIND OF PROBLEMS DO STUDENTS GENERALLY BRING INTO COUNSELING?

Common problems are feelings of self-doubt, feeling shy or uncomfortable with people, difficulties with people at home

---

* The Center referred to is in this instance, of course, the Psychological Counseling Center at Brandeis University.

or on campus, confusion over one's philosophy or choice of one's life work. However, each person is different and therefore has his own unique problems.

DOESN'T EVERYONE HAVE FEELINGS LIKE THAT AT ONE TIME OR ANOTHER?

Yes. However you might ask yourself "How are they affecting me and my relations with others?" "Is my work being disrupted by them?" "How happy am I?" The frequency and intensity of these feelings are an important consideration.

IF I DO POORLY IN A COURSE AND I HAVE SUFFICIENT ABILITY AND INTEREST IN IT, IS IT A REASONABLE INFERENCE THAT I HAVE A PSYCHOLOGICAL PROBLEM?

Yes. Emotions, for example anxiety, may disrupt intellectual functioning. Doubts about themselves often prevent people from working at the level of their ability.

IS IT POSSIBLE TO FREEZE UP IN TESTS AND YET HAVE NO OTHER SIGNIFICANT PROBLEMS BESIDES THAT?

It is possible that this is the only problem of which you are aware. Yet problems are usually not isolated. Some of the emotional attitudes connected with the freezing up may be hidden from awareness.

IS IT TRUE THAT COUNSELING MAKES PEOPLE "AVERAGE," MAKES THEM CONFORM TO THE STANDARDS OF SOCIETY?

It is understandable that a person would be afraid of losing his originality and individuality. However, counseling actually enables the person to make his own choices and to move in the direction which he chooses.

ISN'T IT A SIGN OF WEAKNESS TO HAVE COUNSELING?

Some people do feel that way; this, however, presupposes the idea that counseling takes over. Actually, this isn't so, for the process is far from being a passive one. The student is active in exploring and solving his problems.

APPENDIX

WILL THE COUNSELOR GIVE ME ADVICE?

Although the student and the counselor aim toward solving some problem, advice generally is not given. The most meaningful decisions come from the person himself.

SHOULDN'T A PERSON HAVE ENOUGH WILL POWER TO CHANGE OR IMPROVE HIMSELF?

If it works, that's all right. However, some people try to control by sheer will something which they don't understand. It's difficult to fight feelings or behavior the causes of which are obscure to the person.

WOULDN'T IT BE BETTER TO TRY TO FORGET PROBLEMS INSTEAD OF FOCUSING ON THEM?

Sometimes we do forget experiences, and this may help temporarily. However, if the difficulties continue or reappear this may mean that the forgetting of the problem was not enough. Also, if we forget too much, we may lose control over the very thing which we have tried to control.

I'M ALREADY PREOCCUPIED WITH MYSELF: ISN'T IT BAD TO BE EGOCENTRIC, AND WON'T COUNSELING MAKE ME MORE THAT WAY?

If being preoccupied or egocentric is the result of having unsolved problems on one's mind, then the solving of these problems via counseling should lead to less preoccupation.

HOW CAN TALKING ABOUT PROBLEMS CHANGE THEM?

Talking by itself doesn't change problems. However, talking *out* one's feelings and experiences can lead to seeing them more clearly.

WHAT GOOD DOES UNDERSTANDING DO?

Knowing that one has a problem doesn't automatically do away with it, it is true. However, there are different degrees of knowing. Also, what may appear to be *the* problem, may really not be so basic. Understanding oneself is the *first* step in doing something about a problem.

IS IT TRUE THAT COUNSELING ANALYZES PERSONS BUT DOESN'T HELP TO SYNTHESIZE THEM?

Although it may sound paradoxical, analyzing problems leads to being a more integrated or synthesized person. Analyzing really means exploring and understanding one's feelings and experiences and seeing relationships between them.

I DON'T THINK THAT I SHOULD HAVE COUNSELING BECAUSE I FEEL MY PROBLEMS AREN'T SO GREAT OR WORLD-SHAKING.

Sometimes people feel embarrassed to come for counseling because they think their problems are small or petty. But, no problem is really small if it disturbs a person or detracts from his happiness. Most people who come to the Center are troubled by minor or moderate problems. The Counseling Center would like to try to help students with *any* degree of personal problems.

I THINK I KNOW MYSELF PRETTY WELL. HOW CAN COUNSELING HELP ME?

Many college students do have a high degree of self-knowledge. However, a person may still have "blind spots" or not see the relationship between the different aspects of himself. In that case, an understanding of them can help.

IS IT ALL RIGHT TO COME TO THE CENTER IF ONE HAS NO SPECIFIC PROBLEM BUT JUST FEELS GENERALLY DISSATISFIED OR TENSE AND RESTLESS?

Yes. Disturbing emotions may manifest themselves in such a state, or even in specific physical symptoms and in some cases these are the only manifestations of which the person is aware. One does not have to present a clearly outlined problem to seek counseling help.

IS THE ADMINISTRATION OR ARE OUR PARENTS TOLD THAT WE ARE IN COUNSELING?

No. All contacts are held in professional confidence. If a need for some communication arises, this is discussed with the student.

APPENDIX 131

CAN THE STUDENT START IN COUNSELING AS SOON AS HE MAKES THE DECISION?

We try to see the students as soon as they contact the Center, but it is advisable to start fairly early in the year. If one delays for very long there may be too little time left to get anything done.

HOW OFTEN DO STUDENTS SEE THEIR COUNSELORS ONCE ARRANGEMENTS ARE MADE?

One fifty-minute session each week for as long as seems advisable, but not longer than the duration of the academic year.

WHAT IF THE STUDENT NEEDS MORE HELP THAN THAT?

If it seems that the student needs and could make use of more than one interview each week, arrangements can be made with the help of the Center with an off-campus clinic or psychiatrist. Similar arrangements can be made in those cases where the student at the end of the academic year decides that it would be to his advantage to continue this work for a longer period of time.

There are, of course, many more questions that the student who is interested in counseling may want to ask. He can ask them of the counselor in the first meeting, or discuss them in advance with other people who are well informed about the nature of counseling work, such as the members of the Psychology Department and of the Office of the Dean of Students.